The Law
of Attraction

Made Simple

by

Jonathan Manske

Proudly Published in the USA by
Books To Believe In
17011 Lincoln Ave. #408
Parker, CO 80134

Phone: 303.794.8888
Fax: 720.863.2013

Illustrations by Julia Shuster

JonathanManske.com
BooksToBelieveIn.com

ISBN: 0-9801941-8-0

JONATHAN
MANSKE

Today's thoughts, attitudes
and non-conscious
programming
create tomorrow's results.

~Jonathan Manske

Table of Contents

Part 2: Your Non-Conscious and the Law of Attraction

Appendix

Introduction

I am an expert in the field of human energy and have worked with thousands of people addressing a spectrum of conditions from terminal cancer to the simple headache. I have been working with human energy since 1990 when I lived in the Philippines and studied with an energy-healing master.

Some years ago, in a moment of clarity, I saw that my skills and talents applied not only to the field of health but to all aspects of life.

My ability with energy allows me to look at every aspect of a person's life and business from an energetic viewpoint. Rather than guessing, I can see exactly where a person is in his or her own way of moving forward and succeeding. Often, the people I work with are not aware of these obstacles. Since I am able to see the blocks, I am able to remove them, which frees the person to move forward, to succeed, and to get what they want.

Typical results include: more successful and profitable businesses, greater fulfillment and greater happiness.

The material in *The Law of Attraction Made Simple* comes from my work with real people and their real-life challenges. The tools, tips, and techniques in this book were created in direct response to seeing where people are creating their own obstacles, getting in their own way of getting what they want. Becoming aware of and then having the ability to remove obstacles is essential in making the Law of Attraction work to get you what you want. This material is tried and tested.

I have seen such powerful results from the work I do. I feel that this success is important and I want to share the information with as many people as possible. That is why I wrote this book - to get these tips, tools, and techniques into the hands of as many people as possible - including you.

The Law of Attraction Made Simple is the "how to" of what I do in my private consulting, the work that produces results like these:

❖ A 40% increase in business in two weeks.

❖ Previously unattainable sales goals consistently met.

❖ From worst sales to best sales in 30 days.

❖ Record-breaking athletic performance.

❖ Profound self-acceptance and self-expression.

❖ Increase in overall happiness and well-being.

❖ Dynamic improvements in relationships.

My questions for you are: Why are you reading this book? What exactly do you want to get out of it?

My guess is that you want to improve the quality of your life. You want to get more of what you want, less of what you do not want, and become both happier and more successful.

That is exactly what The Law of Attraction Made Simple is about... you becoming happier and more successful!

My wish for you is that you live a wonderful life, full of joy and happiness. I want you to wake up in the morning excited about the day and go to bed at night happy, fulfilled and grateful! The Law of Attraction Made Simple is designed to inspire and support you to do just that!

Wishing you great joy in your life,

Jonathan Manske

Part 1

The Law of Attraction

Chapter 1

Basics of
The Law of Attraction

The Law of Attraction is a powerful universal law. It affects every part of your life. It is the secret to being happy, living a successful fulfilling life, and having the ability to get what you want. The tips, tools and techniques that are covered in this book are the keys to wealth, health, happiness, success, love and everything else that you desire.

Your understanding of and application of the Law of Attraction relates directly to the quality of your life, your wealth and abundance (or lack thereof) and your degree of success.

Many people measure only one dimension of success: money or wealth. However, real success is much more holistic and includes: financial success; relationship success; career and fulfillment success; physical health and well being; and spiritual success. The Law of Attraction plays a major role in each of these areas!

The Law of Attraction simply states: "You attract into your life whatever you give your attention, focus, and energy to." This is true whether what you attract is wanted or unwanted.

Think of yourself as a large magnet. On that magnet is a control dial, which has settings ranging from crappy to wonderful. Whatever the dial is set for, that is what comes into your life. The dial setting determines the opportunities, the people, the events, the circumstances and the coincidences that show up in your life.

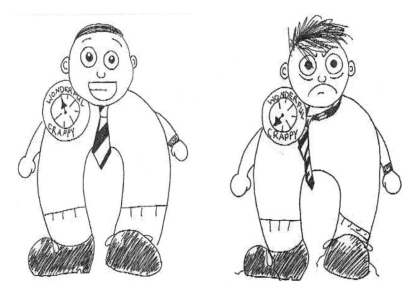

Let us make this analogy a little bit more complex. Think of yourself again as that large magnet but instead of one dial there are many dials. These dials have labels; relationship, money, happiness, health and well-being, career, and so on. It is very possible to have one dial set on wonderful and another set on crappy. All you have to do to see this is look around. You will see people with one part of their life working and another part not working. Said another way, you will see people getting what they want in one area of their life and not in another.

You are that magnet! Your thoughts and feelings, and especially your habitual thoughts and feelings, determine the settings of your dials. If you think crappy thoughts and feel crappy feelings you will attract a crappy life. If you think wonderful thoughts and feel wonderful feelings you will attract a wonderful life. It really can be that simple. Unfortunately, we human beings love to make it much more difficult.

At an energy level here is how that looks:

According to quantum physics, absolutely everything is energy. You are energy. The chair you are sitting on is energy. Your clothes are energy. Your thoughts are energy and so are your feelings.

The concept that "everything is energy" is contrary to our experience. We think we are solid. We think the chair we are sitting on is solid and so on. So, it is important for you to make this leap and keep in mind the fact that everything is energy.

Energy vibrates, and different qualities of energy vibrate at different rates. Energies that are on the same frequency attract each other. They are in a state of resonance. Energies that are on different frequencies repel each other.

Your thoughts and feelings are energy. The energy from your thoughts and feelings penetrates both time and space and in the process attracts and repels. They attract similar energies and they repel dis-similar energies. These energies take the form of people, events, circumstances and coincidences.

One day, I was running just a little bit late for an appointment. I kept thinking, "I do not want to be late." Consequently, I attracted a series of circumstances that had me be late for my appointment. My teller at the bank moved slower than a person coming out of a coma. In my whole life I have never experienced slower customer service. Then I had a moving van actually squeal its tires as it turned in front of me, cut me off and then proceeded to drive 15 mph down the road. About then, I realized what I was doing and had a good laugh at myself. I decided to let go of worrying about being late.

My worry about being late attracted the comatose bank teller and the crazy truck driver.

The quality of your thoughts and feelings directly relate to the quality of your life. Your thoughts and feelings are energy and as such they begin to resonate, attract, and enter into relationship with people, circumstances, opportunities, and events that vibrate at that same rate. When you think crappy thoughts, you attract crap into your life. Conversely when you think positive thoughts, then you attract positive things and people into your life.

Contrary to most people's opinion, getting what you want has very little to do with being worthy, deserving or even earning it. Getting what you want is a matter of you vibrating at the same frequency as that which you wish to attract into your life.

The Law of Attraction is a Universal Law

Have you ever been walking down the street and all of a sudden you start floating up in the air because gravity took a little break? Me neither. That is because gravity is a universal law that is always in effect. It does not matter whether or not you believe in gravity; you are still subject to it. The Law of Attraction is a law, not the "good idea of attraction" or the "wouldn't it be nice if things worked this way principle of attraction". You are always attracting something. You cannot avoid attracting something. The question to ask yourself is: are you busy attracting what you want or are you busy attracting what you do not want?

Since your thoughts and feelings are so important in determining what you attract, you might think that you need to monitor all of your thoughts. However, this would be a very difficult task as we think around sixty thousand thoughts per day. If we evaluated each thought to determine whether it was positive or negative, we would be up to one hundred and twenty thousand thoughts per day. This would be a lot of thinking! It would be an impossible task. Fortunately, there is a much easier way. Your thoughts lead to your feelings; all you have to do is pay attention to how you feel. Even easier, there are only two options. All of your feelings fall into one of two categories:

❖ Some version of feeling good: joy, happiness, confidence, love, peaceful, certainty and...

❖ Some version of feeling bad: angry, upset, sad, jealous, resentful, doubtful...

How you feel determines what kind of magnet you are. Feel good and you are a magnet that is attracting what you want. Feel bad and you are busy attracting everything you never wanted. It really is that simple.

For example, imagine that I want five new clients in my business. So I say, "I want five new clients!" This sounds pretty good. It sounds like I am talking about what I want. But what if I feel bad when I say this? Perhaps I have some thoughts in the background like: "It will never happen." "It is too hard." "I can't possibly do that." Maybe saying it does not feel good, positive or believable. Then what I am actually attracting is the longing for new clients, the disappointment and frustration of not having them rather than attracting what I want, new clients.

Your feelings determine where your dial is set on your magnet, regardless of what you say you want.

Although the principles of the Law of Attraction are quite simple, the application of it is not necessarily so. First, it requires awareness; the awareness to notice how you are feeling and the ability to make distinctions about how you feel. Secondly, it requires the discipline to do something different when you are feeling "bad." It does not matter how right, justified or appropriate your bad feeling is. A bad feeling costs you and has the Law of Attraction work against you. When you truly understand the Law of Attraction, you realize that the cost of loitering in "feeling bad" is costing more than you can afford to pay.

Let us talk more about positive and negative feelings. What if every time you had a negative thought or feeling, an invisible hand slapped you? Would you start to be more selective about your thoughts and feelings or would you just wear a football helmet? Chances are that you would become more selective.

Perhaps it is unfortunate that this slap does not exist because every time that you experience negative thoughts and feelings you are impacting your life in a non-beneficial way. This impact becomes greater the more time you spend in these thoughts and feelings.

How to make this part of your world

❖ Make a point of periodically checking in with yourself and really notice your feelings. Use a timer and check in every hour. You will probably be surprised to notice how often you have negative feelings. Developing this awareness of your feelings will support you with everything else that we cover in this book.

❖ Take responsibility for your life. Realize that the way your life looks right now is a result of your use of the Law of Attraction. The good, the bad and the ugly all came about through the Law of Attraction. Take responsibility for the way things are. Feeling and acting like a victim creates negative energy and will only attract more of what you do not want into your life.

Chapter 2

Change Your Mental and Emotional State

The only thing in this universe that you can control is yourself and specifically your mood, attitude and language. Contrary to popular opinion, you and you alone are responsible for your mood, your attitude, and your state of being. Absolutely nobody can make you feel a certain way. How you feel is up to you!

Your feelings about anything and everything are your choice. Even though these choices have often become habits and orientations, they are still choices you made somewhere in life.

Two people can experience the exact same thing and have two completely different interpretations. That is because the experience itself has no innate meaning in and of itself. The meaning it has is the meaning given to it by the individual.

Imagine that you and I are walking down the street and a kid throws some tomatoes at us. One of us might say, "that little brat should be spanked", the other one might say, "wow it sure looks like that little kid needs some love". The same circumstances happened to us and yet one of us experiences anger and the other experiences compassion.

These different meanings came from each of us individually. We each created our own experience and our own feelings about the situation.

A personal experience I had recently illustrates this really well. My volleyball team had just played badly. After the game I ran off the court and out of the gym. When I came back, one of my teammates was sure that I was mad at her. She thought that I had to run out of the gym because I was so mad about her poor play that I had to get away from her. From my perspective, I ran out of the gym because my bladder was about to explode and I needed to get to the bathroom. I thought that it would be rather embarrassing if I wet my pants.

We had two very different experiences as a result of the same event; me running out of the gym. These two different experiences lead to two very different sets of feelings.

The important thing to realize here is that if either one of us had changed our interpretation, then our perspective and consequently our feelings would have changed as well.

Taking responsibility for yourself and changing your feelings and thoughts when you are upset is one of the most powerful and important things that you can do for yourself.

The important thing to do when you are feeling bad is to change your mental and emotional state. There are many ways to do this. If what you are doing is not working for you, try something different. Remember, how you think leads to how you feel which leads to what you attract. These three are always a match whether we recognize it or not.

Here are a few easy ways to change your mental and emotional state

1) *Change your physical state by sitting or standing up straight and looking up.* People slump and look down when they are feeling bad. Right now slump your shoulders and look down. Notice how your feelings change. Now straighten up, look up and notice how your feelings change again.

2) *Think of someone you love.* You could even picture yourself hugging them. My daughter, Sabine, is four years old. She is extremely cute and charming. Whenever I think about her I experience an emotional change. I can feel my heart open and a smile moves across my face. I become happier. Of course, if she is the one that I am upset with, I should probably think about somebody else, or remember a specific wonderful time with Sabine.

3) *Think about some of the things in your life that you are grateful for.* No matter how rough things

are, you still have things to be grateful for. Focus on those things. One college spring break, my friends and I took a train to Mazatlan, Mexico. The train ride was truly an eye opening experience. I saw large families living right next to the train tracks in nothing more than a tiny shack made out of cardboard. Up to that point, I had never realized how good I have it. My complaints seemed so petty.

4) *Turn on some good music and dance. Get your body moving. Go exercise.*

5) *Sing "If You Are Happy and You Know It Clap Your Hands" or "Don't Worry, Be Happy".* It is almost impossible to remain upset while singing these songs. If you can maintain your upset, I suggest that you explore why you are so committed to being upset.

6) *Make up a different interpretation of the event, preferably one that entertains you.* I lead workshops. One of the facts of the workshop world is that not everyone who promises he or she is going to attend a workshop actually shows up, sometimes even after fervently promising that they will be there. When I was first getting started, this really bothered me. I was counting on them and took their absence personally.

Now when someone does not show up, I trust that they are doing what is best for them. This second interpretation is much easier on me. It leaves me at peace rather than being upset.

Here is how that worked with a client of mine: She had always been a hard working and loyal employee. One day her boss really laid into her about her going behind his back, making him look bad and causing problems. My client was really shaken by these accusations because they were completely unexpected, totally inaccurate and because that is not the kind of person she is.

She was in distress wondering why she had attracted such a horrible event into her life.

After a little investigation, I discovered that she knew that where she was working was not a good fit for her. She was under-challenged, under-appreciated, and ended up spending a lot of time working by herself even though she really likes being around people.

I said to her, "Congratulations for attracting such a strong clear sign into your life that you should not be working there anymore. You are a powerful attractor!"

She tried this interpretation on and she liked it.

Once she felt this new interpretation, the weight of the world lifted off of her shoulders.

If your current state of being is "feeling bad" do whatever it takes to change it now. You can use one of the above methods or anything else that works for you. It does not matter how you change your mood, it just matters that you do change it. If you want to have a great life then you cannot afford to indulge in feeling bad. As my friend Gale Connell always says, "There is never a good excuse to have a bad day." (**CEOSpaceColorado.com**)

The author Johann Wolfgang Von Goethe said, *"Things that matter most must never be at the mercy of things that matter least."* Remember what is important to you.

How to make this part of your world

❖ Pay attention to how you feel. When you are feeling negative do whatever it takes to change that feeling. Use the suggestions from this chapter.

❖ Use a timer to remind yourself to periodically check in and see how you are feeling in the moment.

Chapter 3

Focus

Another way of talking about the Law of Attraction is to talk about focus. What you focus on is what you attract.

A common way that people attract what they do not want is by focusing on the wrong things. Instead of focusing on what they want, they focus on what they do not want. What you focus on expands. So when you focus on your successes you attract more successes and when you focus on your problems you attract more problems.

Another way of saying this is: "what you resist persists". When you resist something, when you say to yourself, "this should not be this way, it should be different", all you are doing is intensely focusing on what you do not want. Thus, you are assuring yourself that you will attract even more of that very thing into your life.

I used to teach a mountain biking class. One of the things I would teach people is how to ride between two trees that are close together. In order to do this successfully, you have to focus on the space between the trees. You have to focus on what you want. As soon as you put your focus on what you do not want, in this case the trees, you will run into a tree.

Class participants would occasionally demonstrate what happens when you focus on the trees. It was not pretty.

How many trees have you hit by focusing on what you do not want?

Our society often focuses on what it does not want. For example:

"Just say NO to drugs!" is a catchy little slogan that is unfortunately flawed to its very core. It contradicts what we know about how the mind works. The word "no" has zero meaning to your non-conscious mind. That part of your mind is a goal fulfilling mechanism that follows the instructions given to it.

The classic example of what happens when you focus on what you do not want is a parent saying to their child, "Billy, don't spill your milk!" What happens so often after that? Billy spills his milk.

In order for Billy to process the instruction about not spilling his milk, the first thing he has to do is make a mental picture of him spilling his milk so that he knows what he is not supposed to do. As soon as he makes that picture, it becomes an instruction for his goal fulfilling non-conscious mind and there you have it, spilled milk.

Here is another example: Do **NOT,** I repeat, do **NOT** think about a pink elephant wearing a yellow tutu. Absolutely do **NOT** think about a pink elephant in a yellow tutu. Remember do **NOT** think about a pink elephant in a yellow tutu.

What is the only thing in your mind right now? Could it be a pink elephant in a yellow tutu?

So back to our flawed slogan, "Just say NO to drugs!" In order to process this instruction, you first have to picture yourself doing drugs so that you know what you are not supposed to do. When you make this picture, it acts as an instruction to your non-conscious to do drugs. Especially if you have done drugs before, this instruction will start certain biological, neurological and chemical processes that are the same as if you took the drug.

Close your eyes and visualize that there is a big fresh juicy lemon right in front of you. Cut that lemon in half and see some of the juice drip out. Now grab half of that lemon, tip your head back and squeeze the juice into your mouth.

What happened? Did your mouth pucker? Mine did while writing this. Certain biological, neurological and chemical processes were started by this imaginary lemon just like certain processes are started by imaginary drugs when you "Just say NO to drugs!"

Are the intentions of the people who created "Just say NO to drugs!" good? Do they want to make a difference and make lives better? Of course! However, they are focusing on what they do not want and making a crucial mistake by using the word, "No." This greatly impacts the effectiveness of the program.

What is the ultimate aim of the war on drugs? My guess is that it is something along the lines of people making better choices and creating better, healthier and more fulfilling lives. I wonder what would happen if the Drug Czar focused on that instead of on war?

If you have money challenges, it is a safe bet that you have been focusing on your problems and challenges with money rather than on what you do want. You have been focusing on the trees rather than the space between them!

People often focus on getting out of debt; they keep talking about their debt; getting out of debt and getting their debt handled. That is not what they really want. They want financial freedom, a healthy relationship with money or... But, they are busy focusing on what they do not want which assures them that they will have more debt in their lives.

Since they are focused on their debt, they will attract the coincidences, the events, the opportunities and the people that will help them stay in debt.

Imagine that you are paying bills and you notice that you are feeling bad and worrying about money. You need to stop immediately!!! Otherwise, you are attracting more bill problems into your life. Get happy!

You could sing, dance, go for a walk, pet the dog or... anything to get happy. Then come back and pay bills from this happy mental and emotional place. If you start feeling bad again, repeat the process.

This is where the rubber meets the road. If you want different results, you need to change! So in this example, if you keep on paying your bills from the same mental and emotional state as you have been, your results are not going to change. Once you change the state that you pay your bills from, there is room for things to change. This requires both discipline and awareness on your part.

A while ago, I was attempting to book a plane ticket to Alaska. I have an attitude about airlines; I do not like the way they do business and think that their customer service is atrocious. Clearly this is not a great attitude. It does not make my life easier, especially when I travel.

I had enough frequent flyer miles on two different airlines to fly for free but neither airline would let me use the miles on the dates I wanted to fly. Another airline had a special for $138 one way but that also was not available for the dates I wanted to fly. So my options were to pay over $700 for this ticket on numerous airlines or use all my frequent flyer miles for a $250 discount and pay $500. Neither of these options sounded very good to me.

Then I realized what I was doing with regard to my focus and the Law of Attraction. Because of who I was being, there was no room or possibility for me to get what I wanted.

So, I stopped searching and went out to dinner with my wife and daughter. When we got home I tried again but with a different attitude, an attitude that I would find a deal that I would be happy with.

I called one of the airlines that I had frequent flyer miles with. This time I got an employee who was interested in being helpful (the other two times I had called this airline they could not be helpful because of my attitude towards them) and he started doing some searching. He found a way I could fly to Alaska for free via LA and a long layover and then Seattle and a short layover. But at least he found something and he put in the effort.

Then I went online to the other airline where I had frequent flyer miles and found a direct flight from Denver to Anchorage at exactly the times I needed to fly that cost me $250 and 15,000 frequent flyer miles. I got exactly what I wanted.

I had been on the phone with this airline several times before and they were even holding two reservations for me but no one had been able to find these flights for me. I had been online at their site several times as well and I was not able to find these flights. I easily found them after I changed my attitude and changed my focus. I changed from having a bad attitude and expecting to have a hard time to a good attitude and expecting to find exactly what I wanted.

In order to get what you want, you have to focus on what you want. But, what about the challenges you have in your life that you are currently dealing with or need to deal with? You know that you cannot just ignore them and hope that they will go away. You have to deal with what you have already created. So how do you focus on what you want and deal with what you need to deal with?

The answer to this comes from the horse world. If you are leading a horse and the horse stops, what you want to do is maintain the same tension on the lead rope and keep looking at where you want to go. If you do this, the horse will soon give in and start following you again.

If you turn around and look at the horse, you have lost and are in for a big struggle. In fact, you just might find yourself going the wrong way. And if you get into a tug of war with a horse, chances are that you have grossly overestimated your strength and are about to experience defeat.

What you need to do is keep focused on where you are going and at the same time keep some of your attention on the horse. The same is true with the Law of Attraction and your issues. You want to keep focused on what you want and at the same time deal with what you need to deal with. The key is to always keep your focus on what you want, on where you are going.

My friend, Wen Boley, has a great technique for creating and maintaining a positive focus in the face of challenges. He uses it to focus on a need without getting needy. (*Hint: Once you get needy, you repel what you want.*)

He has taken his company, StickySheets (**StickySheets.com**) from start up to having distribution in pet stores nationwide in just a few years. His product has won "Pet Product of the Year" and has been featured on the TV program, The View. Along the way he has faced numerous challenges and some very big needs. When you are raising over a million in capital to fund your company, you have some definite big needs.

This is how Wen is able to focus on a need and keep positive energy and feelings flowing: he focuses on the mystery, the mystery of how the universe is going to conspire to bring this about. He does not try to control the "how" or figure it all out. He sits back and watches the "how" with reverence and appreciation. He does not say, "How the heck am I going to do this?" He says, "Wow, I wonder how this is all going to come together?"

Wen recommends that you fall in love with the mystery. Stay curious. This allows you to experience joy in uncertainty. This allows you to maintain a positive vibration, a positive magnet setting even when you have a strong need.

Here is the question to ask yourself: "What am I focusing on?" Do you have a "glass is half empty" focus or a "glass is half full" focus? Most people passionately focus on what they do not want thus assuring that the Law of Attraction will deliver exactly what they do not want.

How to make this part of your world

❖ Take a look at the areas of your life where you do not have what you want. What are you really focusing on? Shift your focus to one that supports you.

❖ Come from a place of happiness, joy and gratitude when paying bills, cleaning the house and so on.

❖ Make a practice of focusing on what you want and being grateful for what you have.

❖ Listen for and then remove the "no" instructions from your life – both in what you tell yourself and in what you tell others. Instead of telling Billy not to spill his milk, tell him what you really want: "Billy, be careful with your glass" or "Billy, move your glass away from your elbow". Change the "no" instructions to clear positive instructions.

Chapter 4

The Formula

Years ago, I entered a rock climbing competition. The whole week before the competition I had this feeling of certainty, I knew in my bones that I was going to win a new climbing rope at the competition. I was also pretty darn certain that it would not be because of my climbing ability. I simply was not that good of a climber and I was going with several people who were much better climbers than I was. Nevertheless, I was certain that I was going to be coming home with a new rope.

After a day of climbing, it was time for beer, barbecue and awards. I walked into the picnic shelter and saw it. There was my new climbing rope. It was a beautiful, white, 60-meter climbing rope lying there on the table just waiting for me.

After everyone grabbed a plate of BBQ and a beer, it was time for the awards. The very first prize awarded was my rope. However, the guy who won it for being the best climber in his division said that since it was his company that donated the rope in the first place it did not really make much sense for him to take it as a prize. He said to put it back on the prize table.

Another guy won the rope for being the best climber in his division. He said that he had just bought a new rope the previous weekend and did not need it. He said to put it back on the prize table.

Then it was time for the door prize drawing. There were a bunch of prizes on the table and all of them were under $20 in value except for my rope, which at that time was worth about $150. It was kind of like that Sesame Street game, "which one of these is not like the others?"

Obviously, there was a bunch of excitement when it came time to draw for the rope. Sure enough, my name was pulled out of the hat and I won my rope.

I was very excited. I thought that this was an awesome experience, and I had no idea how to make it happen again. It was not a repeatable process. However, the formula you are about to learn turns this into a repeatable process, one I have used time and again to win.

Here is The Formula:
Clarity +
    Certainty +
        Activation +
            Letting Go +
                Appropriate Action =
                    The Desired Outcome

The Formula: Clarity

Clarity, or more specifically the lack of clarity, is probably the biggest obstacle people face in their attempts to use the Law of Attraction in order to get what they want.

If you do not know what you want, how can you possibly attract it? There is nothing there for the Law of Attraction to align with. Think how confusing it is for you when someone sends you mixed signals or keeps changing his or her mind. It is the same for the universe.

Imagine going into a restaurant. When the waiter comes to take your order, tell him that you would like some food. After giving you a strange look, your waiter is going to have to ask you to be more specific or else he will not be able to help you. So then imagine that you say you want a salad. After another strange look, your waiter will again ask you to be more specific. "What kind of salad do you want? Do you want the Caesar, the Asian chicken, the spinach or the house salad?" Once you have gotten specific enough then your waiter can do his job and ultimately bring you your food.

When you say, "I would like the Caesar salad with grilled chicken, hold the croutons, and extra dressing on the side", then you have put yourself in a position of being able to get exactly what you want because you have specifically asked for it.

This is exactly what you do with the "menu of life" when you are not clear about what you want. You end up frustrating the waitperson, the abundant universe in which we live, and you end up frustrating yourself because you do not get what you want.

So, step one in the Law of Attraction formula is to get clear on what you want! Get honest with yourself. Dig deep and really question yourself about what you want and then powerfully state what you want.

Your body can be a phenomenal source of guidance in this process. That is because your body is an amazing feedback device. When you are thinking about your goals, dreams, and desires pay attention to your body and how it feels.

If your body feels closed, constricted, flat, or un-energetic when you are thinking about what you want, then either what you think you want does not truly inspire you or else you have a bunch of non-conscious programming that is in your way (we will get to that later).

If your body feels open, vibrant, joyful, or full of energy then you know that you resonate with and are inspired by what you want.

All too often, I see people actively creating non-clarity for themselves. The reason behind this is clarity requires that you do something about it. Clarity can initially cause discomfort or pain.

When you become clear about what you want, you have to admit to yourself that you do not already have it. This can be an unpleasant experience because you have to deal with the reasons why you do not already have it. Next, you have to make a choice: either you start taking the necessary actions to get what you want and become the person you need to be in order to get what you want or you have to start making excuses. So, people will often intentionally keep themselves unclear so that they do not have to deal with this uncomfortable situation.

Chances are, if you say that you do not know what you want, you are purposely keeping yourself unclear.

A great way to create clarity is to spend some time writing down what you want. Set the timer for half an hour, sit down, and start writing about what you want. Take a look at your career, your relationships, your health and well-being, your finances, where you want to be in five years, your big dreams, how you spend your free time, your lifestyle and so on. Write it all down. Then write some more. Allow yourself to dream big and be honest with yourself.

The trick with clarity is to get as clear as you possibly can. Sometimes you will not be clear about the details. In these cases get specific about what you can.

There is a thing I call "sneaky clarity". Imagine that you are looking for a new career but cannot really figure out what you want to do with your life. Even though you are not clear about what this perfect career looks like, you can get clear about some of the specifics. For example: I work less than 40 hours a week. I travel for my job once a quarter. What I do gives me a sense of fulfillment and accomplishment. I work with great people who are fun to be around. I earn $150,000 a year. I have the flexibility to set my own hours. And so on.

Even though in this example you are not sure about the perfect career, there are a lot of details there that you can get clear on and focus on. That is good enough. The clarity you create will lead to greater clarity.

Your job is to get clear about "what" you want. The "how" of getting what you want is handled by God or by the universe if you prefer that term. When you try and control the "how", you get in your own way, you begin to limit the possible ways that what you want can come into your life.

The Formula: Certainty

Once you have gotten clear about what you want, the next step is to move yourself into certainty about it. You have to have certainty that the result you want is truly yours! Without certainty, what you are really attracting is the wanting of the want rather than having the thing itself. Instead of getting what you want, you will attract a state of perpetual longing.

There is a big difference between certainty and belief. Belief exists in your head and in your thoughts. Certainty exists in your body and is something that you know to be true to your very bones.

Belief is overrated and it is especially overrated in the attraction process. Have you ever believed that something would happen and it did not? Have you ever believed that something was impossible and it happened anyway?

What did your belief have to do with what happened?

The answer is, "Not much."

I am not here to smash your beliefs, I think that your beliefs are great and you are welcome to them. However just be aware that they are not as important and powerful as you think they are.

You do not have to believe in order to get what you want. You just need to create certainty.

If you do believe but do not have certainty then you will not get what you want. Of course, you can have both belief and certainty, which is even better.

There are numerous ways that you can create certainty. We will cover two of them here:

❖   The Eight Words That Will Change Your Life

❖   The Wondering Technique.

In later chapters, we will cover two other techniques that also create certainty:

❖   **DIYHTR** (Chapter 18)

❖   Grounding Your Intentions (Chapter 23)

The Eight Words That Will Change Your Life

The Eight Words That Will Change Your Life are: "I can do this and I do it!" The word "this" is like a fill in the blank. "I can have a wonderful relationship and I do it." "I can be a happy person and I do it." "I can attract an extra $10,000 this quarter and I do it." "I can have a career I love and make an excellent living and I do it." You get the idea.

Repeating this phrase with some emotional juice will move you into a state of certainty (certainty not belief). Even if you start in doubt, these eight words will create a state of certainty. These words are like a hammer and chisel chipping away at the doubt until it falls away and you are left with certainty. I can do this and I do it! I can do this and I do it! I can do this…

A variation of this is: I know how to do this and I do it!

The eight words that can change your life come from my friend Joyce Morris *(You can listen to a mini-workshop audio presentation at **LanguageOfAttraction.com**)*. Here is the fascinating story of how Joyce discovered The Eight Words That Will Change Your Life.

Joyce has two pair of twins and the older twins have dyslexia. Joyce decided that the best way to handle the kids' education was for her to home school them.

One day she noticed that the younger twins were learning how to learn from the older dyslexic twins. The younger twins were dyslexic in school but nowhere else in their life because they had learned how to learn from the dyslexic twins. Needless to say, Joyce found this a bit frustrating. She was also frustrated because after several years of home schooling she still did not have a child who could read.

Joyce's background is in education and she had read just about everything you could read about dyslexia and still none of her children could read.

One day Joyce was at her wit's end. She had tried everything she could think of. She turned to one of the older twins, Joe, and said, "Joe, I want you to sit there and say I can do this." To which Joe replied in a slightly tearful voice, "But mom I cannot." Joyce told him to say it anyway and to say it over and over without stopping until it was true.

Joyce likes to say that Joe is dyslexic but not dumb. He knows how to quiet the nagging mother. So he did what she said. He started saying, "I can do this".

Then Joyce had a little insight and realized that there are lots of things we can do that we are not necessarily doing. So, she told Joe to start saying, "I can do this and I do it."

Joe started saying, "I can do this and I do it!" He said this for a while and all of a sudden he got quiet.

Joyce was just about to get on him for stopping when she heard him start to read. For the first time ever Joe read three or four words in a row all by himself.

Joe ended up reading that little book, a second one and got halfway through a third one before he ran into some things he did not know.

By this time Joyce's head was spinning. What was going on here? Could it really be this easy? Why was this not mentioned anywhere in all the material Joyce had read about dyslexia?

They called it quits for the day in home schooling. Joyce was curious to see what would happen the next day.

The next day Joe could not read. Joyce was disappointed but she was not surprised. This was the kids' pattern. They would learn something and then they would forget it.

Then she heard Joe say, "I remember." Joyce thought he was going to remember how to read but instead she heard Joe begin to say, "I can do this and I do it." After Joe said this a couple times he began to read.

From that day forward they never had any home schooling problems unless one of the kids was unwilling to say, "I can do this and I do it."

These eight words work in all areas of your life, not just in home schooling. So even if it is something you truly do not think you know how to do or are able to do, these eight words can move you into the certainty that it can be done. When that happens, it can in fact be done.

Earlier in this chapter, I mentioned that belief is over rated. Joe did not believe that he could read. He read anyway after he used The Eight Words That Will Change Your Life.

My step dad, Ted, loves to fish. Ted and his first wife would spend just about every summer weekend in the mountains fishing and camping. Ted is over 80 now and has a lot of problems with his legs. He does not get around very well and usually uses a walker. Consequently, he has not been able to do much fishing these past few years. When he has gone, he has not been able to go anywhere good because he cannot walk very far or walk over rough terrain.

Last summer my cousin-in-law, Nick, who is the caretaker for a private fishing community in the mountains near Colorado Springs, invited me to bring Ted for a day of fishing.

I was able to drive the car to within eight steps of the water. Ted can easily handle eight steps. Then I helped him into the rowboat and we were ready to go fishing.

At this point, Nick informed me that fishing had not been very good the last week because the weather had been too hot. Fishing had been fantastic when Nick and I set this up. I said, "Well, we are here so we might as well go fishing anyway."

I rowed out into the middle of the lake and we started fishing.

After a little while of not catching anything, I took a look at my feelings. My feelings were something like this: "Oh dear God, please, please, please let us catch something – I am a good guy, Ted is a good guy - please let us catch something." All of that was very whiny.

I started saying, "I can do this and I do it." Every time I said "this" I had a picture in my head of Ted and I catching lots of fish. I kept repeating this and as I repeated it, I began to move from whiny hopeless despair into certainty. Very shortly after that we started catching fish. In the next three hours we caught about thirty trout. It was phenomenal fishing.

There was another boat on this small lake at the same time and they caught one trout.

My use of the phrase, "I can do this and I do it" created an amazing day of fishing for us. Besides the fact that I enjoyed the fishing, there is not a better gift in the whole world that I could have given Ted then that day of fishing. My mother called me the next day to tell me that Ted was still excited.

As I said earlier, your job is to get clear about what you want but not to micromanage the "how." Here is how that worked out: We fished in a different part of the lake than the other boat did. All I did was row out into the middle of the lake and then we drifted to wherever the wind blew us. We did this over and over and the wind drifted us to where the fish were. God and the wind handled the details.

I taught these eight words to a client of mine. She does a form of weightlifting called Super Slow. Super Slow is just like it sounds, super slow. You spend 10 seconds on extension and 10 seconds on contraction. In Super Slow, you go until exhaustion, until the muscle is so fatigued that it cannot do any more.

She started using, "I can do this and I do it" and immediately had a huge jump in the number of repetitions she could do. This is unheard of in Super Slow.

Start using these eight words all over your life and see what happens!

The Wondering Technique

Wonder is an extremely high state of consciousness. You can use wonder to create certainty. When you wonder about the specifics of an outcome, you have already assumed that the outcome will take place. It is a foregone conclusion. You simply do not yet know the details and are wondering about them.

For example, you might wonder who your new client is going to be. You are taking for granted the fact that you will get the new client. You are just wondering who he or she will be. It is a done deal; you just do not know all the particulars yet.

I wonder if the person who buys my house will be single or married. I wonder where the extra $10,000 is going to come from. I wonder who the 50 people in my workshop will be. I wonder how soon this insurance claim will be resolved in my favor. I wonder what the name of my new sweetheart is. You get the idea.

Notice that I am not wondering if something will happen or not. I have already assumed that it will happen and I am just wondering about a detail.

Of course, for this technique to work, you have to get genuinely curious and really wonder about it.

The Formula: Activation

The next step in the Law of Attraction is activation. There are many ways that you can activate the Law of Attraction. You can visualize, take that new car for a test-drive, say your affirmations and declarations, act "as if," make visualization boards, write out your goals, dialogue, and many other techniques. These practices are best done on a daily basis.

In all of these techniques, your feelings have to be involved. You have to feel good about it. You have to "experientialize" it. Otherwise, whatever you are doing is not going to be very effective.

Your daily activation practices repeatedly enter what you want into your non-conscious programming. (We will get to non-conscious programming in Part 2 of this book.) For now it is enough to know that your non-conscious acts as a goal fulfilling mechanism. The activation practices serve as instructions to this goal fulfilling mechanism.

There is quite a bit of overlap between the certainty step and the activation step in that most of the certainty techniques also activate. However, there is no point in activating without certainty. Once you have certainty, activation techniques are something to be used daily and even better throughout your day.

Visualization

Visualization is a powerful way to program your non-conscious mind. It is making pictures in your head of the results you want. You can do this in still pictures, moving pictures, or a combination of both.

You want to visualize exactly what it is that you want to experience in your life. The more precisely you can visualize, the more effective your visualization is. Remember, step one of the formula is clarity. You need to get very clear about what you want. It is very important to visualize what you want rather than what you do not want!

Although you can visualize at any time and in any place, it is a nice practice to turn your visualizations into a ritual.

Here are the steps to doing that:

1)   Find a quiet comfortable place.

2)   Decide on your goal; what you want to focus on in this visualization.

3)   Start creating images around this. For example, if you desire more money, you might visualize yourself getting a bunch of checks in the mail. Then visualize yourself walking into the bank. The tellers all know

and greet you by name because you are in there so often depositing checks. And so on.

4) Make sure that your images are accompanied by strong positive feelings; really experience joy, happiness, excitement and peace.

5) Do this consistently. Even better, do this daily upon awakening and right before going to sleep.

Experiences

Do things that give you a tangible experience of having what you want. You can then draw on this experience in your other activation practices.

For example: Take your dream car for a test drive and really enjoy the experience. Then later on you can replay that experience in your head. You can also imagine that you are driving the car and since you have already driven it, you have a sound foundation for your imagination.

Affirmations

Affirmations are speaking your goals, dreams, and desires out loud or writing them down. Do this in present tense as if you already have them. I have a wonderful relationship. I enjoy driving my new Lexus SUV. I easily and enjoyably make at least $10,000 a month. And so on.

If you say, "I want" rather then "I have" then you are focusing on not having it and wanting it rather than on actually having it. Say the following two statements out loud and notice how different they feel. "I want a great relationship." "I have a great relationship."

As with all activation practices, your affirmations should be done with positive joyful feelings.

Acting "as if"

Acting "as if" is a lot like the WWJD bracelets (What Would Jesus Do?) You step outside of your normal perception of yourself and act differently. Find someone you admire or who you would consider to be a mentor figure. Ask yourself, "What would they do?" and then do that. For that moment be them instead of you.

Ask yourself, "Who would I be and how would I act if I was a marketing genius, if I was in the kind of relationship that I want, if my business was twice as profitable as it is now, if I was deeply happy?" Then do that.

Visualization Board

A visualization board is a collage of pictures, images and words that represent what you want. The idea is to create this and then place it somewhere you will see it every day.

Imagine that you want to get into great shape. Your visualization board might include pictures of people exercising, healthy foods, a picture of a scale reading your desired weight and so on. Find a picture of the body you want to have and then paste your head and face over the one in the picture.

Dialoguing

Dialoguing is the strongest activating tool that I know of. It is a conversation that creates. When you dialogue, you reminisce about a past that exists in your future. You converse with someone (or yourself) about what you want. However, you talk about it as if it has already happened. You are talking about it in the past tense while experiencing the feelings of excitement, gratitude, joy and whatever other positive feelings are there.

Imagine that you know that your friend Bill has some goals to grow his business. Part of your dialoguing might sound something like this:

"Bill, I remember when you set that goal to see 20 clients a week and net $100K for the year. You have got to be just about double that by now."

"Yeah, I remember that too and it really wasn't that long ago when I set that goal. I've more than doubled my goal. In fact, I netted $275K last year and even more importantly I had so much fun doing it. I am truly blessed."

And it just keeps going like that. There is no right or wrong way to do this. The only rule is to talk about what you want from the perspective of having already achieved it.

Imagine that your dream vacation is a trip to Tahiti. Your dialoguing might start something like this:

"Wow Jill, how did you get so tan?"

"I went to Tahiti not too long ago for a three week vacation. It was amazing!"

"How cool is that? What did you like best about Tahiti?"

"That is hard to answer. There are so many things I loved about the trip. However, I did spend about 3 hours a day snorkeling and the water was perfect!"

And so on.

Although at first this might seem kind of silly, it is an extremely powerful technique for manifesting your dreams.

Here is the story I heard about the creation of this technique: A couple really wanted to get a hot tub. However, they did not have the money for it nor was there any realistic possibility for them getting the money to get a hot tub. They decided to try an experiment. They put on their swimsuits, sat on the couch, and pretended they were sitting in a hot tub.

They talked about how good the water felt. They talked about how relaxing the massage jets were. They talked about how soothed and relaxed they felt. And so on.

This whole conversation took place in the present tense as if they were sitting in the hot tub right at that moment.

They did this several times, but then stopped because it just seemed too silly. Not long after this, they were sitting in their real hot tub. Looking back on it, they saw that the process of getting the hot tub started with their conversations of creation.

The great thing about dialoguing is that it is easy. Just focus on and talk about what you want as if you already have it. That being said, here are a few pointers to make your practice even more effective:

❖ Speak out loud, even if you are doing it by yourself. Activate the power of the spoken word.

❖ Your feelings determine what you attract. They are the fuel for your magnets. So bring lots of feelings into the process. Really experience feeling excited and happy and grateful and...

❖ Dialoguing with someone is more powerful than dialoguing alone. However, you are far better off doing this by yourself than not doing it at all.

❖ Support your partner by asking expanding questions that support and enhance their dreams. Ask for details and specifics. Ask them, "What happened next?" and so on.

The Formula: Letting Go

Letting go is as important as any of the other steps. The opposite of letting go is worrying and fretting. A strong attachment to the result is really a doubt that the result can indeed happen.

Attachment can also produce a sort of micro-management, which gets in the way. Your job is the "what". The "how" takes care of itself. You do not need to figure out all of the details or how it is all going to come together.

Think about my climbing rope story. I could have never orchestrated the series of coincidences necessary for me to win the rope. I was just clear about what I wanted and let the details take care of themselves.

Letting go involves the distinction between attachment and commitment. You want to be committed to, but not attached, to the result.

In attachment you identify yourself with the result and probably also with the "how" of the result showing up. It is like flypaper. Once you touch flypaper, it is stuck to you and is hard to get off. Try putting a piece of paper in between you and a piece of flypaper that is stuck to your skin. It is virtually impossible. When you are attached there is no room for what you want to come into your life. Most likely you experience anxiety and other negative feelings, which repel what you want.

In commitment, perspective is maintained. You can pour your belief, your intention, and your power into your commitment. However, you do not identify yourself with the result. By not identifying yourself with the result, you create the space for the result to show up. You feel positive about what you want.

One of the best ways to understand this distinction is to say the two words "attachment" and "commitment" out loud and notice your body's response to them. Chances are that "attachment" will have a sort of unpleasant feeling to it while "commitment" will feel better and stronger.

If letting go is a challenge for you, you might want to turn to Chapter 11, the César Millan Relax Technique. This technique is excellent at helping you let go.

The Formula: Appropriate Action

Appropriate action is an area where people often get tripped up when they are trying to work with the Law of Attraction. The importance of taking appropriate action cannot be emphasized enough. The Law of Attraction is not a substitute for taking appropriate action. The Law of Attraction compliments appropriate action; it makes your appropriate actions more effective! Do what you need to do. Take those steps.

It is vitally important for you to take action on the nudges you receive and on your intuition. These are hints from the universe. These experiences are opportunity knocking. If you ignore the hints you receive for long enough, they will go away.

A joke that I remember from my childhood illustrates this point really well.

It had been raining a lot in a small mountain town. In fact, the town was beginning to flood. The water was already half way up the tires when Bob's friends drove up to his house in their 4-wheel drive. They said, "Come on Bob – let's go!" Bob replied, " Don't worry, God will take care of me. I have been God's good and loyal servant for so long. I will be fine! I built the orphanage. I have done so much. God will take care of me."

Later when the water was nearly up to Bob's second story window, more of his friends came in a boat and urged him to come with them. The result was the same.

Finally a helicopter came when Bob was perched on his chimney top. They urged him to grab the rope ladder because the dam was about to burst. Again, Bob declined and reaffirmed that God would take care of him.

A bit later Bob showed up at the gates of heaven, dripping wet and very annoyed. Before St. Peter had even finished saying, "Hello," Bob complained, "God, why did you let this happen to me? I've been your trusted and loyal servant." Before Bob could continue, a booming voice said, "I sent the Jeep and the boat ..."

I cannot tell you how many times I have picked up the phone and called someone when I had that little nudge to do so. More often than not, the person I called said something like, "I was just thinking about you" or they comment about the perfect timing of the call. Frequently these calls turn into business for me.

There is no substitute for taking appropriate action!

The Law of Attraction and the Law of Action are like your two legs. You need both of them in order to move forward. One leg alone does not get you where you want to go. Try hopping on one leg for 100 yards (a distance you could easily walk) and see how well that works.

People often focus on one or the other. You have the person who is working really hard and not getting the results they want because they are employing a lot of action but have forgotten about the Law of Attraction. On the other hand, you have the person who is sitting on a couch visualizing the success they want and not taking any of the appropriate actions. You need both!

I see this all the time with my clients. A financial planner came to me and said that he was working really hard. He also knew a lot, so he was working smart. Yet, something was out of alignment. He was not achieving the results that he knew he could or even should be getting. What was out of alignment was his improper use of the Law of Attraction.

Remember, you are always attracting something. Sometimes you are attracting what you want and other times you are attracting what you do not want. He was attracting what he did not want.

Once we made some changes in how he worked with the Law of Attraction, the results he was looking for began to show up. His business became much more successful.

Another client of mine wanted more fun, enjoyment and friends in her life. She was doing all of the Law of Attraction stuff but she hardly ever left her house. If she wants people in her life, she needs to go to where there are people. She was out of alignment with her improper use of the Law of Action.

Her life got better once she started getting out of the house.

If I set the intention that I want to become really strong and muscular and all I do is sit on my couch and visualize myself as being strong, some change will probably occur. However, sooner or later, I need to start changing the way I eat and I need to start going to the gym and lifting weights.

Many studies with athletes show that visualization improves their performance. The thing is that while they are visualizing, they are also doing physical training. They are taking other appropriate actions that enhance, support and are synergistic with the visualizations.

Now, if I am eating right, going to the gym, and working out, but in my head I think I cannot do this, or that it is too hard, or something like that - then whatever results I do achieve will be slow because I am fighting myself. Chances are, things will show up to hinder my progress. For example, maybe I will pull a muscle so that I cannot lift weights for a while or something like that.

But if I use both of these, the Law of Action and the Law of Attraction, then I will achieve my goal and I will become a strong muscular person.

Remember, the Law of Attraction is not a substitute for taking action. Habitually lazy people do not succeed!

Somewhere in your life you have probably been told that hard work is the key to success. If this were in fact true, the people who are working two or three jobs to keep their head above water would be tremendously successful. The saying should be that taking appropriate action is half of the key to success and the other half is the Law of Attraction.

This chapter began with my story about winning the climbing rope. Winning that rope was an unrepeatable process for me at that time in my life. But, things do change.

Two summers ago I played in a benefit doubles volleyball tournament. One of the guys in our local volleyball community had a heart attack playing volleyball; the funds raised from this tournament were going towards his medical bills. As part of the fund raising, they were having a raffle for a new portable outdoor volleyball court, which retails for $250.

As I was buying my five dollars worth of raffle tickets, I said to my friend selling the tickets, "Keep selling those tickets since the money goes to a good cause. However, I am going to win."

Then I used the formula. I got clear about what I wanted, the outdoor court. I moved myself into certainty, "I can do this and I do it". I did some activation by visualizing myself winning the net and I also went over to the box and rubbed it a little bit and said "hi". Then I went and started playing volleyball (letting go).

We were just about to start a match when they announced that it was time for the drawing. I said to my partner and to the other team, "hang on a minute,

I have to go win my net." They pulled my ticket for the raffle and I won the net.

The difference between the climbing rope and the volleyball net is that I was able to win the volleyball net consciously and intentionally. I used the formula.

Notice that I did take appropriate action. I bought raffle tickets. Sometimes appropriate action can be a small thing like buying a raffle ticket. Other times there is more to it.

Is it possible that I could have won the volleyball net without buying a ticket? Could I have found somebody's lost tickets on the ground? Of course, this could have happened. But why make it more complicated than it needs to be? Take the appropriate action!

Put an apple in front of you. Without touching the apple try to attract it into your life. Imagine how good the apple tastes, how firm and crunchy it is. Visualize yourself eating the apple. Intend that the apple comes into your hand. Do whatever you can to attract that apple to you.

Once you tire of that exercise, reach out and grab the apple with your hand and take a bite. Which was easier? Which was more effective?

There is a time for the Law of Attraction and there is a time for The Law of Action. The proper use of both will speed your success.

Last night, *(today is the day I finished the rough draft of this book)* I attended a networking event with over 200 people at the Brown Palace Hotel and Spa in downtown Denver. The Brown Palace gave away a complimentary gift certificate for one night's accommodations in a large suite, brunch for two, and two spa treatments. This gift certificate has a value of $1200. Guess who won it?

The lady standing next to me was very excited about the prize and said that she was going to win it.

I said to her, "At these kind of things, I usually win or else the person right next to me wins." Then they pulled my name out of the bowl.

In the past, I was never lucky enough to win these kind of things. Now I win most of the time – not every time but most of the time. The difference is that now I know the formula and I use it to make me "lucky".

How to make this part of your world

❖   Use the formula to get what you want.

❖   Sit down and write a list of what you want. Get as clear as you can. Look at the different areas of your life: career, family, health and well-being, financial, lifestyle and... Then let this sit, come back to it later and see if you can add more clarity.

❖ Use "The Eight Words That Will Change Your Life" whenever you find yourself stuck, up against an obstacle, or in doubt. Use them whether or not you think or believe that you can.

❖ Do some sort of activation technique every day.

❖ When you find yourself attached or holding on to the result, let go! See Chapter 11 for assistance with this.

❖ Use the Law of Attraction and the Law of Action together! Figure out what the appropriate actions are and take them.

Chapter 5

The Deeper Purpose of the Law of Attraction

Imagine that you are at one of my workshops about the Law of Attraction. In this seminar I have taught you **The Formula**. At the end of the talk, I tell everyone to put his or her business card into a hat. I am going to draw out one name and give that person a one on one consulting session with me.

You and all the other people are busy using **The Formula** in order to win the consultation. But, I am only giving away one consultation and I do not draw your name out of the hat. What does this mean? Does the formula not work? Did you do something wrong?

This is a good time to talk about the deeper purpose and meaning of the Law of Attraction.

Much of the current buzz about the Law of Attraction misses the fundamental depth and beauty of this amazing tool. At its essential level, the Law of Attraction is not about getting more and new things. It is about you. It is about a state of being, a state where you love yourself more and relate more authentically with yourself. At its deepest levels, the Law of

Attraction is about you living a great life where you are happy and fulfilled, from the inside out.

Not understanding the deeper purpose of the Law of Attraction is probably the biggest mistake you can make. A trap that people often fall into is thinking that the Law of Attraction is about getting more, new, bigger, and better things. It is not.

Although the Law of Attraction can and does assist us to get things, the deeper purpose of the Law of Attraction is to have us relate better to ourselves, to have us more deeply love, accept, and appreciate ourselves.

Material possessions can certainly be a part of that great life. However, people get themselves into trouble when the material things become their main focus. If you define yourself by the things you have, you will never truly be happy. There will always be something else you need in order to be happy. If you define yourself by your inner state of being, you can truly be happy. You can be a happy person who, by the way, also has the big house, the new car and the nice things.

When the things become your main focus instead of your state of being; your happiness and quality of life will suffer. Your happiness becomes dependant on things and circumstances that are external to you. Consequently you lose your centeredness and your peace of mind. Your life will go better when you keep this in mind.

Think about it. Why do you want to attract more, new, bigger, and better things into your life anyway? The answer is because you think that it will make your life better and you will become happier. But, you know of people who have lots of things and are not happy. You probably also know people who do not have very many things and are happy. So it is not the "things" that make you happy, it is how you relate to them.

Make being happy your top intention and your ability to attract what you want will naturally follow.

This speaks to something even bigger. God created our world. *(Note: if the word "God" does not work for you then substitute a word that does work for you.)* Everything is God. All there is, is God. Whether you have lots of money or no money; that is God. Whether you are successful or not; that too is God. Whether you win the free session or you do not, that too, is God. One is not better than the other.

When you really get this, you also understand that everything is perfect and that you are being everything you need to be in this moment. So from this place, love yourself. Experience the magnificence of your being.

So back to the drawing for the free session with me: If in using **The Formula**, you had fun and even deepened your relationship with yourself, then you were also a winner.

Clarity about what you really want also comes into play here. Chances are that what you really want is the value that you would get from our consultation rather than the experience of us working together. What if the input you want comes from another source rather than from the free session with me? Remember, God will manage the details of fulfillment. Maybe you will get what you need from overhearing a random conversation. Maybe you will cross paths with me later and we will have a conversation. Maybe you will open a book and there you will see exactly what you need. There are a million other possibilities.

One other point to remember, the Law of Attraction is a natural law and so is the Law of Timing. The moon waxes and wanes. Season follows season. Babies grow inside their mothers for nine months before they are born. Seeds take time to grow and some seeds grow faster than others. So, even if what you are attempting to attract does not show up lickety-split that does not mean that it is not on its way.

It would be pretty silly to plant a garden and then dig it up every day to check on how the seeds are doing. You have to have a certain amount of trust that the seeds are going to do what they are supposed to do. Meanwhile you need to do what you need to do like: water, weed, and fertilize your garden. You need to have some patience!

How to make this part of your world

❖ Remember the Law of Timing. Seeds take time to grow. Keep on with your practices and be patient.

❖ Remember at its deeper levels the Law of Attraction is about you loving and appreciating yourself. When you do not love or appreciate yourself, stop! Actively take steps to love and appreciate you (more on this in Chapter 7). You will be using the Law of Attraction to improve the quality of your life. The biggest change you can make that will improve the quality of your life is to love and appreciate yourself more.

Chapter 6

"What" not "How"

Your job in the Law of Attraction is to get really clear about "what" you want and to let go of the "how". The "how" is God's job or the universe's job.

My friend, Mattison Grey (**GreyStoneGuides.com**) has a great analogy for this. Imagine you decide that you want to go to California. You are totally clear that you want to go to California. It does not really matter how you get there. You could drive, fly, hitchhike, walk or bike. The thing that matters is that you get to California. The rest is just details.

Do you remember how Superman is affected by kryptonite? A normally unstoppable person (faster than a speeding bullet, able to leap tall buildings in a single bound and so on) becomes totally weak and helpless in the presence of kryptonite.

That is the way "how" works for most people. It stops them. It weakens them. It is their kryptonite. Is it your kryptonite?

It is important to distinguish between a curious "how" and a kryptonite "how". A curious "how" – "Wow I wonder how this is going to happen; I wonder how I can accomplish this?" moves you forward. A kryptonite "how" – "I don't know how to do this!" stops you dead in your tracks.

The "how" is to just take that next step, to take action on nudges and inspiration. There is an immense amount of wisdom in the old saying about how a journey of a thousand miles begins with a single step. Oftentimes you cannot see the "how" you cannot possibly see the whole path. However, you can always see the next couple of steps – so get walking.

Here is another great old saying that relates to getting stopped by "how": Inch by inch life is a cinch; by the yard it is hard.

Remember, the universe takes care of the "how" through coincidences, serendipity and synchronicities. We just have to take care of the "what". We do that by becoming very clear about what we want.

Imagine that you want to attract an extra $10,000 into your life within the next three months. That is pretty clear. If you start adding "how to" details, you start to limit what is possible. For example, if you say that the extra $10,000 comes from a new client then you have eliminated numerous other possibilities for money coming into your life and have limited it to just this one possibility, a new client. Now it is much more difficult for that money to make its way into your life.

Synchronicity and Coincidence

It is always fun when you notice synchronicity and coincidences showing up in your life. The more that you listen to and act on intuition and nudges, the more that synchronicity will show up in your life. The more often that synchronicity shows up in your life, the easier your life will get.

I believe that the only reason our lives are not completely full of synchronicity is that we get in our own way. We live in an abundant universe that is just waiting to fulfill our desires. We just need to get out of the way and let this happen.

Remember my story about winning the climbing rope. I got myself out of the way and let the "how" take care of itself. I could have never scripted all those coincidences that resulted in my coming home with a new climbing rope.

Also remember, appropriate action is very important in this process. I never would have won the rope if I had not acted on the nudge to go to the climbing competition in the first place.

Those nudges and intuitions are the universe talking to you, setting up the "how to" of bringing you what you want.

I heard a great story about Deepak Chopra and coincidence. Prior to takeoff, Deepak started a conversation with the man next to him on the plane. The man's phone rang. Since they were sitting right next to each other, Deepak overheard the conversation between this man and his wife. She wanted him to pick up a book at the bookstore on his way home.

After the man finished his phone call, Deepak asked him what his wife's name was. Deepak then opened his briefcase, took out a copy of his book, The Spontaneous Fulfillment of Desire" and autographed the book for this man's wife. This was the book that she had requested her husband pick up on his way home.

When you act on those nudges, hints and coincidences, magic will show up in your life.

How to make this part of your world

❖   Take action when coincidences and miracles show up in your life.

❖   Act on the nudges you receive. For example if it pops into your head to call someone, call them.

❖   Listen to that inner voice of intuition and then act on it.

❖   Take the next little step regardless of whether you can see the whole path.

Chapter 7

Habitual State of Being

As you know, your thoughts and feelings determine what you attract. There are thoughts and feelings in the moment and then there are habitual states.

Your habitual state of being is an incredibly crucial piece in your ability to attract what you want. This key is almost always overlooked. What are your habitual mental and emotional states?

Where do you live on the happiness scale? Where do you spend the most amount of time?

1 ——————————— 5 ——————————— 10

Gloom & Doom   **Happiness & Joy**

If your habitual state of being is a five or below, you are going to have a hard time attracting what you want into your life. Your day-to-day living counteracts the attraction work that you are doing. Metaphorically you are swimming against the current, which is hard work and results in very little progress.

Swimming against the current is a great choice for a workout. It is a really poor choice for getting somewhere. You will just end up tired and having not gone very far.

If your habitual state is above a five then you are naturally in positive attraction. From this place, applying the tips, tools, and techniques of attraction that you are learning here will create rapid success.

What you need to realize is that happiness is a choice not a result! This is so important that it is worth repeating: **Happiness is a choice!** You can be happy for no other reason than because you choose to be happy, regardless of the circumstances.

Here is a story that illustrates this really well:

A 92-year-old man had to move into a nursing home. His wife of 70 years had recently passed away which made his move necessary.

After several hours of waiting in the lobby of the nursing home, he was told that his new room was ready. The person guiding him to his new room started to describe the room.

"I love it!" He stated with the enthusiasm of an eight-year-old with a new puppy.

The person who was leading him to his room said, "we haven't got there yet just wait."

"That doesn't have anything to do with it," the old man replied. "Happiness is something you decide on

ahead of time. Whether I like my room or not does not depend on how the furniture is arranged. It's how I arrange my mind. I have already decided to love it!"

"It's a decision I make every morning when I wake up. I have a choice; I can spend the day in bed recounting the difficulty I have with the parts of my body that no longer work, or get out of bed and be thankful for the ones that do."

"Each day is a gift, and as long as my eyes open, I'll focus on the new day and all the happy memories I have stored away."

~source unknown

Why do you even want to attract new and better things into your life? Most likely you believe that having these things will make you happier. However, you know people who have what you want and are not happy. So happiness is not necessarily in the having. You can choose to be happy with what you have and you can choose to be unhappy with what you have.

If you are habitually living at a five or below on the happiness scale, the work that lies before you is to: **Get Happy — Be Happy — Stay Happy**. That should be your number one priority.

Imagine that there is a light switch right in the center of your chest. This switch has a label on it. It says, **"HAPPINESS"**. Flip that switch on right now!

Feel the happiness begin to flow through you. Experience feeling happy simply because you choose to. Practice this frequently!

The more self-love you experience, the happier you are. The happier you are, the easier it is to attract what you want into your life. The more you love yourself, the better your life gets.

Take a minute and imagine what it would be like if you could completely, totally and ecstatically love yourself? What would that really be like? What will your life be like when you deeply love and appreciate yourself?

Here are two easy ways to enhance your self-love:

❖   Wrap your arms around yourself and give yourself a big hug. Really hug yourself and whisper to yourself, "I love you!" Say it like you would to a sweet little child. Do this several times a day. Even better, do this while looking yourself in the eyes in a mirror. (Note: I do not recommend doing this in public unless you really enjoy having people look at you strangely.)

❖   When you identify one of your challenges, issues, or problems, repeat this statement to yourself for a couple of minutes: Even though I _____, I deeply love and appreciate myself! For example: Even though I procrastinate, I deeply love and appreciate myself! Even though I have this money issue...

The greatest gift that you can give to yourself, your family, friends, and to all of humanity is to love yourself and be happy. Happy people do not start wars. They do not hurt and abuse others. They do not go around causing pain.

People often have issues with loving themselves because they think that they are defective, not good enough, or messed up in some way. "If I just change this one thing, then I could love myself." "If I did not procrastinate then I could love myself." And so on.

If you think that you are not okay or that you are imperfect, you are mistaken. That is your illusion. Who you are and the way your life is right now, is perfect for this moment in time. It cannot be any other way. You are a part of God and God is perfect!

Let us explore the word "compassion". Self-compassion is a wonderful thing to have. Compassion can be broken down into two words: common and passion. Compassion is seeing and experiencing what you have in common with all of humanity.

The whole human experience exists inside each one of us – the good, the bad, the ugly, the beautiful, and the wonderful. It all exists inside of you.

Your little quirks, peculiarities, problems, challenges, strengths and skills are all part of the common human experience. The only thing that is unique about you is your particular mix of these things.

Think of the weirdest thing that you can. Chances are there is a name for it. There would not be a name for it if it were not a shared part of the human experience. There are lots of people who share your "unique qualities".

These are the "unique qualities" that you use to separate yourself and that you use to put yourself down and beat up on yourself. But, your "unique qualities" are just part of this experience of being alive here on planet earth. They are not that special or unique and they certainly are not worth beating yourself up over. Make peace with this and your ability to love yourself will increase.

How to make this part of your world

❖ Lighten up and enjoy being alive. Be grateful for your life as it is right now.

❖ Daily set your intent to be a happy person. "My habitual state of being is an eight on the happiness scale (a scale from one to ten)."

❖ Choose happiness. It really is a choice and you can choose it. Choose to be a habitually happy person. When you are experiencing not being happy; choose to be happy. Choose to experience happiness in that experience. You have the power to do this.

❖ When you are experiencing not being happy use one of the two techniques to enhance self-love.

❖ Practice turning on the happiness switch in the center of your chest. Do this frequently.

❖ Love and appreciate yourself daily. Make it a practice. Create a habit or ritual around this!

Chapter 8

Life Purpose

Many people spend a lot of time wondering about their life's purpose. They believe that when they discover their life's purpose, they will be happy.

This is just another example of the deceptive thinking that goes, "when I get that one thing then I will be happy". As we have already covered, happiness is a choice – regardless of what you have or do not have.

Ironically, this is completely backwards. Your life purpose is to be happy. You bring happiness or lack of happiness to what you do; you do not find it there.

I heard a story about someone asking the Dalai Lama about life purpose. He replied that your purpose in life is to be happy.

People often think that this seems too whimsical or insignificant. They need a *real* life purpose, something important and relevant, something they can sink their teeth into. Get over it! Your life purpose is to be happy. That is what will make this world a better place.

Happy people do not live a life of crime. Happy people do not abuse other people. Happy people do not go around creating problems and disharmony. They treat others well and go around spreading happiness. This world needs your happiness.

Of course, your path to happiness is going to be different from mine and from that of your best friend and so on. What is it that makes you happy? What really and truly makes you happy? The more of what makes you happy that you have in your life; the easier it will be for you to attract what you want.

How to make this part of your world

❖　Dwell on this for a minute and really get this: Your purpose in life is to be happy!

❖　Every morning, set your intent to live a happy life and to experience happiness in your daily life.

❖　Explore – what is it that really makes you happy?

Chapter 9

The Law of Attraction Paradox

The paradox of the Law of Attraction is that in order to get what you want, you first have to be okay with what you already have. If you are not okay with the way things are now, if you have not accepted them and made peace with them, then you have effectively trapped yourself into staying right where you are. As Carl Jung said, "What you resist persists."

This is another way of talking about focus. If you are busy resisting something, if you are busy saying, "this is not the way things should be" then you are focusing on what you do not want. What you focus on expands. This means that you are cementing in the very things that you do not want when you argue with reality.

In order to move forward, you must first be okay with where you are now.

Let me illustrate this with a metaphor. Imagine that you want to drive to LA and you are in San Diego. However for whatever reason, you will not admit to yourself that you are in San Diego, and in fact insist that you are in San Francisco. So you start driving south and instead of ending up in LA you end up in Mexico.

You have ended up being somewhere you do not want to be because you were not okay with where you were. As silly as this sounds, you have done this before. People do it all the time.

Even though it is sometimes a little painful to be honest with yourself about where you are, it is well worth it. Being dishonest with yourself does not serve you, does not assist you in achieving your goals, and does not make your life better.

There is a great book by Byron Katie called *"Loving What Is"*. She talks about dealing with what is so and loving what is. There is a lot of wisdom in this concept. If you have not read this book, you might want to.

It takes a lot of energy and effort to argue with reality and to either deny or twist what is in front of you. Yet, people do this frequently. They live in a state of denial, which greatly impacts their ability to attract what they want.

Healing addictions is a great example of this. The first step is always to get the addicted person to see and then admit that he or she has an addiction. Once they have done that, then there is a possibility for healing to occur. Until they admit this, there is zero possibility.

The thing is, we are all addicts. There are certain thoughts and feelings that you are definitely addicted to. These addictions determine where the dial on your magnet is set. If you deny that you are addicted in the first place then you are going to remain stuck where you are.

For example: If you are addicted to anger, you will attract people who do stupid things around you so that you have something to be angry about.

A client of mine wanted his life to become easier and simpler. He looked at his life and realized that he was addicted to adrenaline rushes. Once he saw that, he was clearly able to see how often he made things much harder than they needed to be in order to get that adrenaline rush that came from accomplishing his tasks. He was in the habit of adding complication and rush to his life.

Once he saw it, he was then able to do something about it. He is much more relaxed these days.

Gratitude

One great way to become okay with the way things are right now is to use gratitude. Get grateful for what you have and for the lessons and opportunities that are before you right now. No matter what your situation is, there is something in it to be grateful for. Focus on that thing and really experience gratitude.

Most likely, the gratitude will lead you to see that where you are right now is perfect. Ironically, this now frees you up to move forward.

Make a list of all the things that you have to be grateful for. Just start writing. As you write more and more things will come to you.

When you wake up and before you go to sleep, spend a minute on gratitude. I cannot think of a better way to start and end your day.

I was focusing on gratitude one day. As I was being grateful for my house, I had a great experience. I suddenly realized just how much I really like my house. It is a perfect house for us. Previous to this, my deep liking of my house had existed outside of my awareness. I had never consciously realized just how much I liked my house. Doing the gratitude exercise made me present to the fact that I really like my house. This "awakening" provides me with numerous opportunities to experience joy simply by walking in my front door.

Here is a great statement to keep in mind: Focus on what you want and be grateful for what you have. This will put you in a position to easily attract what you want.

How to make this part of your world

❖ Focus on what you want and be grateful for what you have.

❖ Practice gratitude. Even in the darkest of times, there is always something that you can be grateful for.

❖ Start and end your day with a couple minutes of gratitude.

❖ Learn to see the blessings and the gifts in your current situation. Then be grateful for these blessings and gifts. Ask yourself, "What is the gift, what can I learn from this situation?"

❖ Take a look at your life and see where you are saying, "This should not be this way!" Stop resisting what is and come to peace with what is. Only then will there be room to experience change.

❖ Identify your mental and emotional addictions. Once you have identified your addictions, you can do something about them. *(Hint: What thoughts and feelings frequently come to mind? What do you day dream about?)*

Chapter 10

The ABC's
of Attraction

ABC stands for Always Be Celebrating! What you focus on expands. When you focus on your successes and celebrate your successes, you are attracting more successes into your life.

Do you downplay your accomplishments? Do you take yourself for granted? How often?

Most likely the answer is *A LOT*. Cut it out! Start to celebrate yourself and your accomplishments!

It is so easy to do something and then just be done with it rather than celebrating the accomplishment. At first it might seem a bit odd to pump your fist and go "woohoo I just cleaned the bathroom". Try it anyway for a day and see how much more energetic and enthusiastic you are by the end of the day.

What about the things you do well, do you celebrate them? Do you allow yourself to be "wowed" by yourself? If you are a janitor, do you look at the floor you just cleaned and say to yourself, "Wow, way to go! Look at the floor sparkle!"? If you are a financial planner do you say to yourself, "Wow I just did fantastic work with that client!" and pat yourself on the back? If you are a housewife, do you say to yourself, "Wow that was an excellent dinner I cooked for my family. Way to go!"?

Or are these just things that you do and while you do them well, they are everyday and therefore not notable?

These things are worth celebrating. Start celebrating them now. Get a sore shoulder from patting yourself on the back.

Do you celebrate your major accomplishments? Chances are that unless you are able to fully celebrate your minor accomplishments, you will also be unable to fully celebrate your major accomplishments.

When you do not celebrate these major milestones, you are shortchanging yourself. You are ripping yourself off from experiencing satisfaction, fulfillment and joy. You are also cheating yourself from receiving an energy boost that recharges you.

Think of a recent accomplishment right now. Feel how good that feels!

I played doubles volleyball in the sand with three friends earlier today. I played well. In fact, as we rotated partners, I ended up having the most wins thus making me the king-of-the-beach for the day. When I think about that accomplishment, I feel energy start to flow through my body and I find myself smiling. Then it is time to let go and move on.

Before you go to bed at night think of five successes that you have had that day and spend a minute patting yourself on the back. Be "wowed" by yourself! Do this with genuine feeling. Even better, develop the habit of celebrating these successes as they happen, in the moment.

There is so much about yourself that you can celebrate when you start looking for it. Every breath, every heartbeat is a miracle. You could celebrate those. What about the wonder of listening to your body tell you it is hungry and then feeding it? Wildly celebrate yourself!

Some people worry that if they do this they will turn into an arrogant, self-absorbed person. Unless you already are that, you won't.

The trick to celebrating yourself without turning into an idiot is to celebrate and then let go and move on. If three days later you are still celebrating the peanut butter and jelly sandwich you made, you probably have an issue here.

Use celebration to enhance the quality of your life and to turn up the dial on your attraction magnet.

How to make this part of your world

❖ At the end of the day look back and see some of your successes. Pat yourself on the back for a job well done and really experience your self-acknowledgement, really let it in.

❖ Acknowledge yourself for doing a good job even on the things that you habitually do well.

❖ Allow yourself to be "wowed" by yourself!

❖ See and acknowledge the successes in others and you will start to see more of your own successes.

❖ Ask yourself, "What is so great about me?" Then answer the question.

Chapter 11

Cesar Millan Relax Technique

Cesar Millan is known as the dog whisperer. He does amazing things with dogs and their problem owners. The problem is almost always with the owner not the dog.

In his TV show, Cesar shows up at someone's house and the owner expresses disbelief that Cesar will be able to do anything with the problem dog. Then Cesar takes the dog for a walk. When he comes back from the walk, an obedient, relaxed and well-mannered dog is following at his heals. The owner is always astonished.

The way I see it, what Cesar does is he gets the dog un-fixated. Imagine that there is a dog that barks at people passing by. Cesar puts a training leash on the dog and then has his assistant start to walk back and forth on the sidewalk in front of the dog. Every time the dog barks, Cesar gives the leash a quick jerk and says, "Tsssssss Relax! Relax!" It is not long until the fixation is broken and the dog does not even pay any attention to the person walking by. Again the owner is astonished and the dog is happier without the fixation.

When Cesar says, "Relax," he is not asking the dog if maybe it would kind of like to relax if it does not mind. He is speaking with certainty and strength and also from love. He knows that the dog will relax. He is telling the dog to relax right now and that is exactly what he expects.

What does Cesar Millan and problem dogs have to do with you? Inside your head you have both the dog and the owner.

You have three brains inside your head: the reptilian, mammalian and neocortex.

The reptilian brain has the same type of archaic behavioral programs as snakes and lizards. It is rigid, obsessive, compulsive, ritualistic and paranoid. This brain controls muscles, balance and autonomic functions, such as breathing and heartbeat. It is active, even in deep sleep.

The mammalian brain is concerned with emotions and instincts, feeding, fighting, fleeing, and sexual behavior.

The neocortex possesses the higher cognitive functions, which is what distinguish humans from animals.

The neocortex allows you to observe yourself, to comment on what you are doing, and give yourself instructions. A dog cannot do any of these things.

When you are upset, stuck or fixated, you can do to yourself what Cesar does with these dogs. You can tell yourself to relax and get yourself un-fixated. You can "jerk your own chain" and tell yourself to relax.

Try it now. Several times, say out loud, "Tssssssss. Relax!" and see what happens.

You will relax. You will become calmer, more centered, more resourceful, and able to see a bigger picture. All of these things help you attract more of what you want.

This technique is especially useful if you find yourself trying to control something that you have no business trying to control – like other people.

This technique is also really useful if you have challenges with the "letting go" part of the formula for attraction. "Tsssssss Relax. Let It Go!"

I taught this to one of my clients and she really put it to use. When I saw her again a week later she looked different. Her face was softer and more radiant. She looked more beautiful. She said that her friends had been asking her if she had gotten a haircut or had lost weight. They could tell that something was different they just could not put their finger on what it was.

What was different was that she had become more relaxed and peaceful. She had stopped trying to control a lot of things that were outside of her control. She said about her new more peaceful state, "This is not who I know myself to be, but I kind of like it." She was no longer a control freak (her own term) and this change happened from using this technique.

In a very short time she became happier, had a big jump in career and income success, and got out of a relationship that was no longer a good fit for her. Not bad from a little "Tsssssss relax!".

You can use this with other people as well. Remind them to relax. Their initial response often times can be a little irritated – kind of like, "who are you to tell me to relax" but then it usually sinks in and they relax. My wife usually gives me the evil eye first when I say to her, "Tsssssss Relax!" and then she relaxes and lets go.

Using the Cesar Millan Relax Technique can change your mental and emotional state in just a few seconds. When you change your state you change the dial setting on your attraction magnet.

When you hold on to things like anger, upset or other bad feelings, you get in the way of your ability to attract what you want. The Cesar Millan Relax Technique can help you release what you are holding on to.

Think about an issue you have or maybe somebody that you are annoyed with. Feel where this sits in your body. Feel where you are holding this in your body. To that place in your body say "Tsssssss Relax, Release, Let It Go!" Breathe it out as you exhale.

You will feel it let go. You might need to say this to yourself several times in order to fully release it.

Your body is a wonderful feedback mechanism. Pay attention to it and it will show you where you are holding on to things that do not serve you. Tune in to that area and let it go, release it! Tsssssss Relax!

How to make this part of your world

❖ Use the Cesar Millan Relax Technique. Use it frequently. Use it when you are stressed, worried or anxious. Use it when you are having challenges in letting go.

❖ Tsssssss Relax!

Chapter 12

Money, Compliments & Acknowledgement

In order to get what you want, you have to be able to receive it! Try going to a restaurant and order some food. When your server is about to put the food on your table say, "Oh no, I do not need that, you keep it." You are going to end up very hungry and frustrated. Sound familiar?

On a scale of 1 – 10, how good are you at receiving compliments and acknowledgement? When you resist and deflect these, you are preventing what you want from coming into your life.

Think about it this way. Money is just another form of acknowledgement. When you pay someone, in effect here is what you are saying, "I acknowledge that the service or product you provided for me is useful and valuable, let me give you some of my money."

When you dodge acknowledgement, you are making it harder for money to find you.

Do you know someone like this? Are you someone like this? "Yeah I did drag 15 people out of that burning building – but it was not any big deal any other person would have done the same thing." But it was a big deal because it was YOU who did it! So celebrate that it was you who did it and let in the acknowledgement.

This is back to not taking yourself for granted like we talked about in the ABC's, Always Be Celebrating. Be "wowed" by yourself!

The other day I was talking with a friend of mine who is a chiropractor. She was having a hard time accepting compliments about how good her work was and taking credit for some of the really amazing success stories that her clients have experienced. She said, "Yeah but, other chiropractors could have done the same thing."

Now while this may be true, that other chiropractors could have produced these results, she is the one who did produce these results. She is the one who went to chiropractic school. She is the one who has taken hundreds of hours of advanced study after she was already a chiropractor. She is the one who has been working on, improving and refining her technique for years. She is the one who marketed to these people and attracted them into her business. Therefore, she is the one who is responsible for producing these great results!

Really getting this and owning it will make a big difference for her. It will make her more attractive to success and to money.

Another client of mine is also a chiropractor. The first time we worked together we identified a block in his business. The block was his ability to receive appreciation. He said, "People tell me all the time that I have changed their lives but I do not really get it."

If he could not let in their appreciation, then he could not really let them in. If he could not really let his clients in then it would be hard for those clients to come to his office. If they do not come to his office the likelihood of them writing him a check are pretty small.

We shifted this dynamic and he could immediately connect with that feeling of appreciation. He could feel it in his body. Within two weeks his business had grown by 40%. We created this shift using **DIYHTR** (Chapter 18).

Our society gives us lots of messages that make it harder for us to receive compliments. Do not draw attention to yourself. Keep a low profile. Do not toot your own horn. Be modest. And so on.

What these messages do is have people discount and downplay their own magnificence. This results in false humility.

False humility is not pretty. It inhibits self-expression and authenticity. It has you play small and settle for less. This in turn limits your ability to ask for what you want which severely limits your ability to get what you want.

I love this quote from Marianne Williamson:

"Our deepest fear is not that we are inadequate. Our deepest fear is that we are powerful beyond measure. It is our light, not our darkness that most frightens us. We ask ourselves, Who am I to be brilliant, gorgeous, talented, fabulous? Actually, who are you not to be? You are a child of God. Your playing small does not serve the world. There is nothing enlightened about shrinking so that other people won't feel insecure around you. We are all meant to shine, as children do. We were born to make manifest the glory of God that is within us. It's not just in some of us; it's in everyone. And as we let our own light shine, we unconsciously give other people permission to do the same. As we are liberated from our own fear, our presence automatically liberates others."

Embrace your own magnificence and at the same time be objective. Neither false humility nor over the top boastfulness will get you what you want.

Think of the people who are generally admired for their strength of character. Typically they possess a quiet assuredness and a strong sense of who they are. They exude genuineness. They are not trying to be someone they are not. At the same time they are comfortable with who they are and what they have achieved.

How does it feel when you acknowledge someone and they blow it off? It is kind of disappointing. You had something that you really wanted to express and the other person did not take it in. Why would you do that to someone else when they compliment you?

You want to build up your ability to receive. Here is how you do that. When someone pays you a compliment, you just let it in as deeply as you can and then say, "Thank you." That is it. You do not need to compliment them back, just let it in and say, "Thank you."

The other day my daughter said, "Daddy, I love you." My initial response was to say, "I love you too Sabine." Instead I paused, let it in, and then said "Thank You". I felt great afterwards. Her words really sank in and touched my heart. I had little man tears in the corner of my eyes. How cool is it that this sweet, cute, smart, wonderful little girl loves me! If I had not paused to let that in, I would have ripped her off from being able to give me that gift and I would have ripped myself off by not being able to receive that gift.

Also learn to compliment yourself.

Referrals are appreciation as well. If your business depends on referrals and you resist receiving compliments and acknowledgement, then you make it harder for people to refer you. You stand in your own way of receiving referrals.

How to make this
part of your world

❖   Get over your false humility programming. Own and embrace all the good things that you are and all the good things that you do.

❖   Receive compliments as graciously and as deeply as you can. Let them in and say Thank You!

❖   Get in the habit of complimenting yourself.

Chapter 13

The Language of Attraction

Language and how it relates to the Law of Attraction could easily be a book unto itself. However, I would be remiss if I did not at least touch on it here. Paying attention to and then making some changes in your language is a very valuable thing that you can do for yourself.

Your words, both those spoken aloud and those spoken silently; often outside of your awareness have everything to do with what you attract. Who you are is nothing more than the network of conversations that you are having with others and especially with yourself. How you talk about your life makes an enormous difference!

Language is the paintbrush by which you paint what is real for you. People mistakenly think that they are reporting on the way things are with their language when what they are really doing is creating. Every time you speak, you are having conversations of creation. You speak your reality into existence.

When you talk about something from your past, you are not reporting about it. You are recreating it.

This has been proven in scientific study after scientific study. On a hormonal, chemical, neurological and energetic level your body responds exactly the same to these stories from the past as they do to something happening in the present. What kind of stories are you telling yourself and telling about yourself?

In the May 22, 2007 issue of The New York Times, there is an article by Benedict Carey entitled, *"This is Your Life (and How You Tell It)"*. It states that through interviews with hundreds of men and women some trends became very clear. People with similar life issues were telling similar stories.

"During a standard life-story interview, people describe phases of their lives as if they were outlining chapters, from the sandlot years through adolescence and middle age. They also describe several crucial scenes in detail, including high points (the graduation speech, complete with verbal drum roll); low points (the college nervous breakdown, complete with the list of witnesses); and turning points. The entire two-hour session is recorded and transcribed.

In analyzing the texts, the researchers found strong correlations between the content of people's current lives and the stories they tell. Those with mood problems have many good memories, but these scenes are usually tainted by some dark detail. The pride of college graduation is spoiled when a friend makes a cutting remark. The wedding party was wonderful until the best man collapsed from drink. A note of disappointment seems to close each narrative phrase.

By contrast, so-called generative adults — those who score highly on tests measuring civic-mindedness, and who are likely to be energetic and involved — tend to see many of the events in their life in the reverse order, as linked by themes of redemption. They flunked sixth grade but met a wonderful counselor and made honor roll in seventh. They were laid low by divorce, only to meet a wonderful new partner. Often, too, they say they felt singled out from very early in life — protected, even as others nearby suffered."

Listen to yourself.

How often do you talk about your problems?

How often do you talk about what is not working?

How often do you talk about what you do not want?

Every time you engage in one of these activities you are ordering exactly that from the menu of life. Instead of ordering what you want, you are ordering what you do not want.

When you catch yourself talking about what you do not want, ask yourself what you do want instead.

When you catch yourself talking about problems and about what is not working ask yourself, "What do I like about this? What is good about this?"

I went on a trip with an old friend of mine. Not long into our road trip I noticed a disturbing trend. She always found something wrong with whatever it was that we were doing. When she did this, she would suck the fun right out of the space.

We were sitting on top of a small mountain that we climbed near the highway rest stop. I was enjoying the view, the fresh air, the sunshine, the chance to stretch my legs and the physical exertion of climbing this little mountain. After sitting there for a few minutes, my friend said, "Do you know what I do not like about this?"

I snapped. I said, "I do not care what you do not like about this. I do not want to hear it. Do not even try to tell me because I will not listen. Tell me what you like about it."

This surprised her a bit. Once she got over her shock, she told me what she liked about it. From then on whenever she started to talk about what she did not like, I asked her what she did like. Not surprisingly, our fun-o-meter went up.

Your choice of words matters as well. Although synonyms have the same meaning, they can have very different impacts and repercussions.

Say these two words out loud: "money" and then "capital". Feel the difference in your body. Chances are that the word "capital" felt a lot lighter, more friendly and happier. Even though these two words have essentially the same meaning, they have a very different impact. The word "money" has an eighty-car freight train of baggage behind it that the word "capital" does not have.

Learn to pay attention to which words expand you and which contract you. Then be selective in the words you choose. One of my clients constricted around the word "wealth" but not around the word "abundance". She will be much better served by talking about "abundance" rather than "wealth".

Remember, feelings are the fuel of the Law of Attraction. If you are using words that constrict you then you are creating feelings of constriction, which will attract constriction into your life.

Say these two phrases out loud: "I need you" and "I want you". Can you feel the difference? The word "need" both constricts and repulses.

Yet how often do you talk about needing something? When you think that you need it, you actually repulse it. And the truth is that you do not need it. You might want it but you do not need it.

Here is the short list of what human beings need. Everything else is a want.

❖　　You need oxygen to breathe on a very regular basis.

❖　　You need to eat again within the next 40 days.

❖　　You need to drink water on a regular basis.

❖　　You need to be able to maintain a certain body temperature range through clothing, shelter and/or a heat or cooling source.

That is it. Without those things you die. Everything else is a want. When you talk about a want as if it was a need, you confuse things. The next time you catch yourself saying "need" add the words "or else I will die" to the end of the sentence and see if it still makes sense.

"Hurry up we need to leave now" becomes "hurry up we need to leave now or else I will die" which sounds a little silly.

As much as possible speak in terms of "want to" rather than "need to". Even better, use "choose to".

The words "I choose" are two of the most powerful words that you can speak. Just as need constricts, choice expands. Say these two sentences out loud and feel the difference. "I need to go to work today." "I choose to go to work today."

Language Pitfalls

Here is a list of some of the things that people do with their language that gets in their own way. Listen to your language and see which of these common errors you are making.

Being unspecific: You need to be clear and specific about what you want. If you say that you want more money and I give you a penny, you have got more money. However, this is probably not what you had in mind.

Micromanaging the details: Your job is the "what" not the "how". As soon as you start trying to control the universe, you get in your own way. Your clue here is when you hear yourself talking about "how".

Talking about what you do not want: What you focus on expands. The more you talk about what you do not want, the more of that you attract into your life.

Pressuring words: There is always a backlash to using words like "should", "must", "need", and "have to". Try "I choose to" instead.

Using words that do not work for you: There are going to be certain words that just do not work for you for whatever reasons. These words might be fine for someone else but these words have a negative meaning for you and cause you to constrict. An example of this is the lady who constricted on "wealth" but not on "abundance".

Say "savings" and see what you notice. This is a word that does not work for most people. If you are saving then there must be lack that you need to save against, which means that you are focusing on the lack. Yet you probably have savings accounts at the bank. Give this account another name and see how that feels. Call it your financial freedom account or your money growth tool or …

Self-judgment and talking bad about yourself: Any time that you criticize yourself or call yourself names, you are changing the dial on your magnet towards attracting what you do not want.

It amazes me how often I hear somebody say something like, "Geez, I'm so stupid" or much worse. Beating up on yourself does not make your life better, nor does it change the behavior you are beating yourself up over in the first place.

Having a "fixing" orientation: Chances are that if you need to fix something then there is a problem. And if there is a problem, chances are that you are focusing on the problem rather than on what you want.

Rather than trying to fix something, intend to attract joy and happiness into your life. This is a matter of shifting your focus.

Here is an example to illustrate this: Imagine that you have debt and that you view that as a problem to be fixed. When you shift your focus off of the debt and on to something like intending to experience joy around money, you have moved out of trying to fix something. Instead you are creating something powerful for yourself.

A friend of mine is a real estate investor. She owns several rental homes. One of her homes became vacant at the same time that she was experiencing a cash flow crunch. She needed to get some repairs done to the house, did not have the cash available to pay for the repairs, and was not very excited about the prospect of doing them herself.

She was focusing on her problem, her need to get her house repaired. She caught herself doing this and switched her focus to experiencing joy in getting her house repaired. Within a day of doing this her doorbell rang. It was a laborer she had used in the past who was looking for some work and his rates were pretty cheap.

She immediately put him to work. However, after a day of work he vanished. When she called him, he apologized but since the snow had melted his boss called and he was roofing houses out in the plains of Colorado.

Since the work was already started, she decided to just go finish it herself. She packed up her tools and her kids and headed off to her rental house.

Not long after they started working, she began to notice some strange things. Her teenagers who were painting in the other room sounded like they were having a really good time even though they hated painting. She also noticed that she was having a really good time repairing the drywall, which surprised her.

It got to be quitting time and she said to her family, "I promised you a pizza so why don't you all go home and get a pizza. I am actually enjoying this so I am going to stay here and work a while longer."

Her son said, "You know what mom, I am having fun too. Why don't we get a pizza sent here also and I'll stay and help you."

Everyone else agreed that they were having fun as well. They got the pizzas delivered to the rental house and kept on working into the evening.

That is when it hit her. She was experiencing joy and her house was getting repaired. The way that it was happening was not a scenario that she would have ever imagined but nonetheless, she got what she desired.

Remember, the "how" and the details are not your job!

Your use of language is your power to create. You can have a wonderful magnificent life right now if you declare your life to be that already.

Say, "I have a wonderful magnificent life!" How does that feel? You already do have a wonderful amazing magnificent life, right now, and it is in your power to realize that and affirm that.

How to make this part of your world

❖ Really pay attention to your language. Notice how you use language to support yourself and how you use language to create obstacles. Notice how you use language to attract and how you use language to repel. Change your language and see how your experience changes.

❖ Upgrade the conversations you are having that do not support you to conversations that do support you.

❖ Pay attention to the stories you tell. Do they make your life better or worse? Are there common themes?

❖ Use words that work for you and avoid the words that do not work for you.

❖ Listen for and avoid the common language pitfalls. Talk about your goals and desires while having somebody else listen for these pitfalls. They will hear where you are making these mistakes and are not even aware of them.

Chapter 14

Talk Nice to Yourself

Do you pay attention to the way you talk to yourself? When you start to do this, it will make a big difference in your life.

There is an old saying about how you would not let somebody talk to you the way you talk to yourself in your head. When you badmouth yourself in your head, there is a cost. In fact, there is a tremendous cost.

One day a friend of mine decided to say everything out loud that she was already saying to herself in her head. By the end of the day she looked horrible. She looked pale and worn out. She was absolutely shocked by the sheer number of not nice and even downright nasty things she said to herself, about herself.

After this little experiment, she started talking nicer to herself. Not surprisingly, she got happier.

How you give yourself instructions is an important area of self-talk to explore. The specific words you use create or at the very least flavor your experience.

If you use words like: "I must", "I should", "I am going to put my nose to the grindstone now", "I have to", and other phrases of this nature, you are putting pressure on yourself. Every time you put pressure on yourself, there is a part of you that rebels against that pressure. Thus, you are getting in your own way. You are creating your own resistance.

The only thing that thrives on pressure is a tire. Now, you might be one of those people who says, "but wait, I use pressure all the time in order to produce results." Notice that I used the word "thrive". Yes, you might be producing the results but not in a way that takes care of you. There is a huge cost to producing results this way.

Your natural response to pressure is to resist and to push against it. This requires both energy and effort on your part, which is energy and effort that is no longer available towards reaching your goal.

Usually this happens because people have not made the distinction between pressure and intensity. Pressure is a force applied from the outside. Intensity is a power that comes from within you. Pressure is a force that is forcing you to do something that you might not want to do. Intensity is compelling focused desire that naturally moves you forward.

Try talking to yourself using words like: "I choose to", "I prefer to", or 'I want to". Have a "steps toward my dream list" rather than a "to do list".

As long as you are choosing, you might as well choose to have fun. Make fun a part of your intention.

"I choose to have fun preparing my taxes."

"I choose to have fun while I fix the leaky faucet."

"I choose to have fun in my relationship."

"I choose to have fun while I am stuck in traffic."

"I choose to have fun while growing my business."

You get the idea. Choose fun and-surprise surprise, you will have more fun in your life! As long as you are doing whatever it is that you are doing you might as well have fun.

The other day I had a speaking engagement across town. The highway traffic was backed up to approximately forever because the rain from the night before had clogged a storm sewer. There was a lake beneath the overpass and one lane of the highway was underwater. Rush hour and a closed lane are never a good combination.

I noticed I was saying to myself, "This sure is not fun." In that moment, I chose fun. I chose to have fun regardless of the circumstances, simply because I said so. Then I set my intention on arriving on time.

I arrived with thirty seconds to spare.

The most important thing is that I arrived in good shape. I was peaceful and relaxed because I chose fun rather than going with my first feelings which were stressed out, anxious, and worried about being late. As you might imagine, peaceful and relaxed is a much better place to deliver a talk from than stressed out, anxious and worried.

Imagine that somebody is making you go through an obstacle course and that you do not want to do it. "I have to get over this stupid wall." "Ouch, that hurt!" "Crap, now I've got mud in my shoe and I am wet." You have a whole lot of not having fun.

Now imagine that you are at the obstacle course again except that this time you want to be there. You probably will not even notice the bumps and bruises you are accumulating until after you have crossed the finish line. Then the scraped knee, bleeding forearm and wet muddy shoes just make crossing the finish line that much more rewarding. You can smile and laugh about your wounds and see them as medals of accomplishment.

In both examples, it is the same obstacle course. The only difference is the attitude in which you approach it.

There is a semi-annual event in England's West Midlands called the Tough Guy Competition. It is an 8-mile race through mud, manure, water, fire, barbed wire, nets, electrical shocks, smoke grenades, sewer pipes, underwater tunnels, ice, ropes, cables, and tires. People pay money to do this and they have fun doing it. About 5,000 men and women participate in this event twice a year. (**ToughGuy.co.uk**)

Mud, manure, fire, barbed wire, the possibility of broken bones and hypothermia do not exactly sound like a recipe for fun. Yet, these people have fun because they choose to do so. Some of them even survive and come back time after time.

One April 15th, I got up at 3:00 am to do a lot of supposedly tedious stuff to get my taxes together. Before I started, I set the intention that I was going to have fun doing it. The amazing thing is that I did indeed have fun — doing tax prep of all things. It was kind of strange when I looked back and saw that pretty much the whole experience was enjoyable. It was not as fun as going to Mardi Gras but it was fun. I enjoyed doing some organizational type activities that I usually do not enjoy doing.

So the choice is yours. Obstacles can be fun or they can be a pain in the behind. What determines this is how you talk to yourself about them.

How to make this part of your world

❖ Notice if you are putting pressure on yourself with your words. If you are then stop! Start using different words.

❖ Replace words like: should, must, have to and need with "I choose to".

❖ "I choose" might be the two most powerful words in the English language. Use them often.

Chapter 15

The Magic of Intention

Intention is your access to magic and miracles. Your intention serves as the template for creation to occur. Your intention creates the setting for the magic of the universe to line up behind. Having powerful clear intentions is absolutely key to effectively using the Law of Attraction to get what you want.

My favorite story about the power of intention is Sir Ernest Shackleton and the Endurance. Shackleton was a polar explorer. One of his expeditions was forced to turn back just 97 miles from the South Pole or else he would have been the first person to make it to the South Pole. Before he could try again, Roald Amundsen reached the pole.

Shackleton then set his sights on becoming the first person to cross the Antarctic continent. In Shackleton's own words, "After the conquest of the South Pole by Amundsen who, by a narrow margin of days only, was in advance of the British Expedition under Scott, there remained but one great main object of Antarctic journeyings—the crossing of the South Polar continent from sea to sea."

In 1914, Shackleton and his 27 men set out on the Trans – Antarctic Expedition.

The pack ice was heavier than normal that year and Shackleton's ship, The Endurance, became trapped in the ice about 200 miles from where they planned to make land fall and begin crossing the continent.

Spring was seven months away at this time so Shackleton knew that his expedition was going to have to spend the Antarctic winter trapped in the ice. He knew then that his biggest job was to keep morale from crumbling. He had seen that too often before in other expeditions and knew that the loss of morale lead to death.

Ten months after The Endurance was beset by ice, she was crushed by the shifting ice and sank. Shackleton and his men were forced to abandon ship and live on the ice pack.

At this point, Shackleton knew that his goal of crossing the continent was no longer achievable and he said that if he could not cross the continent, then he would bring all of his men home alive. Shackleton said, "Ship and stores are gone, now we go home."

This was an extremely bold prediction because polar exploration and death often accompanied each other in those days.

Keeping up morale became even more important at this point. Many say that it was Sir Ernest Shackleton's sheer willpower that kept his men from cracking. He had the strong intention that he would bring all of his men home alive.

They lived for five months on the drifting ice. At one point the ice split right under a tent and one of the men dropped into the water while he was still in his sleeping bag. Immediately after he was pulled out of the water, the ice slammed back together.

After five months of living on the ice, the ice became unstable and started to break up. The expedition was forced to take to three lifeboats, the biggest of which was only 22½ foot long.

They spent seven miserable days in these boats before they landed on Elephant Island. Men's hands froze to the oars. There was repeated danger of being capsized by whales. The conditions were harsh. It had been one year and four months since they last touched land.

However, Elephant Island was not much better. It is a small, exposed, storm raked island in a corner of the ocean where nobody goes. Their chances of being found by a passing ship were virtually nonexistent.

The ship's carpenter modified the biggest of the three boats, the James Caird, to make her more seaworthy. Using scavenged wood he raised her sides a couple of inches, gave her a canvas deck and equipped her with a sail.

Then Shackleton and five other men set out on probably the most insanely dangerous sea voyage ever. Their goal was to sail 800 miles across the world's most dangerous ocean in a 22½ foot boat and make land fall on the island of South Georgia.

South Georgia is a small island in the middle of nowhere that had a whaling station. If Shackleton and his small crew missed South Georgia, they would certainly perish at sea.

During the voyage, they were only able to use their sextant a few times in order to navigate. The rest of the time the weather was too rough and they were forced to navigate by dead reckoning. Dead reckoning is the process of estimating one's current position based upon a previously determined position, or fix, and advancing that position based upon known speed, elapsed time, and course. In other words, they were doing a lot of guessing. And they were guessing where the stakes were extremely high. One small error and they would never even see the island of South Georgia. They would die at sea.

At the end of their 17-day voyage, with South Georgia Island in sight, they were hit by a hurricane that they had to fight for nine hours until they could make landfall.

Initially, they were euphoric that they had made it. After the euphoria wore off, they realized that they were on the opposite side of the island from the whaling station.

Three of the men were unfit to move and the James Caird was unfit to go back to sea. They could not sail around the island. Their only option was to cross South Georgia by foot. However, no one had ever even entered the interior of the island before. The middle of the island was uncharted terrain filled with peaks, glaciers and crevasses.

Shackleton and two others set out on foot for the whaling station that was 22 miles away. They had a compass, screws from the James Caird sticking out of the soles of their boots for traction, a carpenter's adze and 90 feet of rope. They also had a strong drive to succeed. Shackleton said, "Over on Elephant Island 22 men were waiting for the relief that we alone could secure for them. Their plight was worse than ours. We must push on somehow."

After 36 straight hours of hiking, they walked into Stromness Station. At one point they were trapped on a high peak and took a big risk by blindly sledding down on their butts.

That afternoon after they arrived at Stromness Station, a blizzard hit. If the blizzard had hit while they were still trying to cross the island, they would have been killed.

From here it took four tries before Shackleton was able to make it back to Elephant Island and rescue his men. The ice thwarted the other three tries.

All of the men were alive! They had survived on Elephant Island for 105 days.

All of these miracles started with Shackleton's iron clad intention to bring all of his men home alive.

This quote by Goethe is often connected with the story of Shackleton and the Endurance:

"Until one is committed, there is hesitancy, the chance to draw back, always ineffectiveness, concerning all acts of initiative (and creation).

There is an elementary truth the ignorance of which kills countless ideas and splendid plans: that the moment one definitely commits oneself, then providence moves too.

All sorts of things occur to help one that would never otherwise have occurred.

A whole stream of events issues from the decision, raising in one's favor all manner of unforeseen incidents and meetings and material assistance which no man could have dreamed would have come his way. Whatever you can do or dream you can, begin it. Boldness has genius, power, and magic in it. Begin it now."

– Johann Wolfgang Von Goethe (1749-1832)

Goethe's quote talks about committing. Intention is committing to the result. "I will bring all my men home alive!" The climbing rope story is the same process, different stakes, life versus a climbing rope, but the same commitment to the results. "I will come home with a new climbing rope!"

The intention is not about the "how". It is about the end result. Shackleton and his men experienced miracle after miracle after miracle as the "how" took care of itself. As Goethe said, "... then providence moves too."

There is intention and then there is **INTENTION**. These two are not the same

Intention without any power, commitment or heart behind it is just a wish. "Wow, it sure would be nice if this happened." True intention has power, commitment and heart behind it. It is being at cause in your life and saying, "I intend to bring this into being". You are drawing the proverbial line in the sand and stepping over it.

There is an expression about throwing your hat over the wall. Once you have thrown your hat over the wall then you are forced to climb over the big scary wall in order to get your hat back. You are now committed to producing the result whether or not you have any idea how to do it or even if you are not sure that you can.

When you use intention nothing really happens. When you use **INTENTION**, miracles happen.

I do public speaking. When I give a talk without a strong intention, I seldom get the results that I want.

When I do set a strong intention like, "I will generate business out of this talk" I get the results that I want.

Start to play more with intention in your life. Set strong intentions and see what happens. See how your intentions can shape your physical reality.

Many scientific studies have shown that intention produces a physical result. See Lynne McTaggart's "The Intention Experiment" or Dean Radin's "The Conscious Universe" and "Entangled Minds".

William Tiller Ph.D., the head of the Material Sciences Department at Stanford, conducted some interesting experiments. If you want to dive into scientific language, you can read about them in his paper, *Exploring the Effects of Human Intention and Thought Energy*.

Tiller had a group of meditators hold a specific intention for ten to fifteen minutes. They directed the intention to an item in another laboratory that was two thousand miles away. The intentions were: changing the pH of water, changing a chemical ratio in fruit fly larva, and increasing the thermodynamic activity of a liver enzyme.

The meditators' intentions affected the items in a way that is considered to be a very robust result.

Tiller proved, in a scientifically valid manner, that intentions are able to affect the physical world.

Tiller says, "These are very remarkable results that are certain to confound our physics, biology, and medical colleagues; however, the experimental data speaks for itself in spite of the entrenched belief systems held by others."

As I was writing this chapter, I thought, "I need a good story about intention". That evening I went to an event where I ran into one of my clients. She pulled me aside and told me her story.

She needed to hire a new part time person who would be responsible for answering the phones. She needed this new person sooner rather than later.

She posted the job online and in just a few days she had about one hundred responses. She sorted through these responses and ended up with twenty-five people who made her "A" list. However, none of these "A" listers made her say, "Wow! This is the person I want."

She was tempted to settle for one of these people, as she needed someone right away. But then she said to herself that she was going to find the right person and she was going to do that today.

Shortly after that, the phone rang. It was someone who was wondering if her company was hiring. This person did not know about the job posting. The job seeker had heard about the company through a mutual friend and thought that it sounded like a good fit. So, she picked up the phone and called my client to see if they needed anyone.

This job seeker made my client say to herself, "Wow! This is the perfect person for the job. I want her."

I got what I wanted. I got this story, and my client got what she wanted. She got a new employee, from setting a strong intention.

Imagine that you and I tie a few logs together, push them into the river and jump on our new raft. Once on board, we are pretty much at the mercy of the current. We will be forced to go where the current takes us whether that is smooth water, into the branches of an overhanging tree or over a waterfall. This is how most people do life.

Now imagine that we have a long pole, some paddles, or a rudder. Now we have some say about where we go in the river and what parts of the river we experience. This is what intention does for us in the "river of life".

One day I was playing Robert Kiyasoki's Cash Flow board game with some friends. I was having horrible luck. I had gone bankrupt several times and I was getting irritated. I realized that I was not paying attention when I rolled the dice. I was not looking ahead and then setting my intentions. I was just rolling the dice and taking whatever came. Once I started paying attention and then started setting intentions, my "luck" turned.

This was also eye opening for one of my friends. It never occurred to him to set intentions when he rolled the dice. He just took whatever came. He noticed this is what he did in his life as well.

How to make this part of your world

* Set strong intentions and act with purpose. Set an intention for your day every morning.

* Notice when you are just drifting in your life, taking what comes and begin to set your intentions. Even if you set one intention it will make a difference.

* Watch either "The Endurance: Shackleton's Legendary Antarctic Expedition" or the PBS movie, "Shackleton" with Kenneth Branagh.

* In Chapter 18, we will cover **DIYHTR**. You will learn a technique that will make you more effective in using intention.

Chapter 16

Do You Really Want What You Think You Want?

A majority of people have lost the ability to know what they really want and to then ask for it. The more that a person loses his or her vitality and aliveness, the less in touch they are going to be with what they really want. The aliveness and vitality of most adults has taken a serious hit.

Compare yourself to a healthy child. Do you have the same amount of vitality and aliveness as that child? Chances are, your answer is no. This means that your vitality and aliveness have been diminished, which means that you are going to be less in touch with what you really want.

The relevance of this is if you are busy trying to attract something you think you want, and at deeper levels you want something different, you will be in conflict with yourself. Consequently, you will have a heck of a time trying to attract what you think you want.

If you have been trying to attract something and it is not showing up in your life, you might want to take a look at whether or not you really want what you are trying to attract.

Mattison Grey (**GreyStoneGuides.com**) has created an incredibly simple and very powerful way to create deeper clarity about what you want.

1) Imagine that you have/achieved what you want.

2) Ask yourself, "What will I do next?"

3) Take your answer from number 2 and ask yourself, "What will that cause?"

4) Take your answer from number 3 and ask yourself, "What will be different?"

Going through these four steps will have you be much clearer about what you really want.

You can repeat this process several times to see if you can drill even further down into what you truly want. *(Hint: Usually what you want at these deeper levels is a state of being like being peaceful, happy, experiencing love, or something like that.)*

Here is a real life example of this process:

My client's goal was to have a successful business. So, he imagined that he had achieved having a successful business.

His answer to "what will you do next?" was that he would do more of the same except on a bigger scale. He would work with bigger clients, fortune 500 clients across the globe and world leaders.

"What would that cause?" He would feel like he was doing what he was put on the planet to do. He would feel complete, whole, fulfilled and satisfied.

"What will be different?" He would be at peace with himself.

Having a successful business and being at peace with himself are two very different goals. He was focusing on a surface goal yet what he really wanted was something much deeper, to be at peace with himself.

Seeing this and then switching his focus was an important step in his life. Almost immediately, he became more at peace with himself.

When you get clear about what you really want then you are being true to yourself. When you are not being true to yourself, you will end up fighting yourself and will most likely have problems attracting what you think you want.

Ironically when you are being true to yourself it becomes much more likely that you will also be able to attract the more superficial goal as well.

One of my clients owns a fairly good-sized company, over 200 employees, and she has done quite well for herself over the years. However, recently she has been facing some challenges. Some of the company's systems and departments are under-performing and there is some legal issues going on with the company.

We were talking about what she wanted with regards to her company. She said that she wanted to get the under-performing systems and departments up to speed and she wanted to get the legal stuff handled.

After a little probing, what became clear was that she wanted to fall in love with her company again. That is what she really wanted. All these things had happened causing her to fall out of love with her company, and become tired and disinterested.

Once we brought this to light and she got clear, she experienced a big change. She felt lighter, happier and immediately more interested in her company. This is because she connected with her true desire rather than what she mistakenly thought she wanted.

If you are having challenges in getting what you want or in taking action around what you want, you might want to probe a little deeper and see if what you think you want is indeed what you really want.

How to make this part of your world

❖ Take your goals, especially those that do not seem to be moving forward and apply Mattison's clarity process.

Part 2

Your Non-Conscious and the Law of Attraction

Part 2

Have you ever seen a picture of an iceberg? The ice that is visible above the surface of the water is only a small portion of the iceberg. The vast majority of the ice is out of sight under the water.

The same is true for the Law of Attraction. Most of what you attract is determined by what is beneath the surface. It is determined by your non-conscious programming.

Therefore, it is absolutely essential for you to understand a little bit about the non-conscious and more importantly, to have some tools to change your non-conscious programming.

Part two of this book teaches you how to look and work beneath the surface in order to be able to attract what you want into your life.

Chapter 17

Your Non-Conscious is Really in Charge

If you are like most people, you think that you are in control of your own life. You think that you are in charge. You think that you make logical rational decisions that direct the way your life turns out. You think that you are awake and aware.

If you think this way, you are mistaken! Most of what is going on happens outside of your conscious awareness.

Your non-conscious programming is the single biggest factor that determines the way your life looks right now. Science has proven that 97% of the way you perceive the world, which leads to the way you think and behave, is an automated non-conscious response. In other words, you have programming that has you be who you are.

The good news is that when you change this programming, you can change who you are and you can change your life.

This can be a little challenging to grasp at first because we think that we are awake, aware and in charge. But, the truth is that we are not. The following example will give you a taste of this.

Imagine that the most attractive person you have ever seen in your whole life is walking towards you right now. You can predict right now how you are going to respond in this situation. Whether you run away in fright, pretend that you do not see the other person, ask him or her out on a date, or... your response will not come as a surprise to you. That is because your response is your programming that says, "This is what I do in the presence of a really attractive person". It is automatic. You do not have to think about it. The programming shows up instantaneously and directs how you interact with the really attractive person.

Your whole life is made up of this sort of programming. Programming that says:

> This is who I am.
> This is who I am not.
> This is what I believe.
> This is what I do not believe.
> This is what I do in this situation.
> This is what I do in that situation and so on.

The majority of the thoughts you think and the actions you take every day are nothing more than a knee jerk reaction, an automated response.

Even though your response is automatic, you can bring your conscious awareness to the situation and then do something different. Let's say for example that around really attractive women, I look down at the ground and try to be invisible. That initial response occurs but then I can say to myself, "Hey Jonathan, make eye contact with her and say hello". It might not be easy for me to say "hello" since I am going against my programming but I will probably be able to do it – or maybe I will not be able to do it.

Have you ever made cut out Christmas cookies? If you use the Santa Claus cookie-cutter, the only kind of cookies you can make are Santa Clauses. You cannot make a reindeer with the Santa Claus cookie cutter. You cannot make a Christmas tree with the Santa Clause cookie cutter. If you want to make something different you need to get a different cookie-cutter.

This is a great analogy for the way your non-conscious programming works. Your programming determines what you can experience out of all that is possible for human beings. If an experience lies outside the boundaries of your programming (outside your cookie-cutter) you will not be able to experience it unless you change your programming.

Computers make another great analogy. Can you write a letter using Excel? Can you edit a video using Word? Of course not! These programs allow you to do certain things and to not do other things. To do these other things you need different programs.

The majority of your non-conscious programming came about by accident. There is no personality store where as an infant you went shopping. "I would like some charming, a box of worry about money, and hey, is that impatience over there, give me a bunch of that."

Much of your non-conscious programming came from your experiences with parents, teachers and other influential people. It also came from what you saw and experienced. It came from what you have been taught and what was modeled out for you. Much of your programming was established in childhood.

Your self-image (the image inside your head of who you are) and who you have defined yourself to be are nothing more than the sum of your non-conscious programming. There is no absolute truth; no absolute "this is who I am". Who you are right now is simply an accumulation of past experiences that have become your current truth. This can be changed! Just like you can change the programs (software) on your computer, you can change your mental programming.

Maxwell Maltz was a very famous plastic surgeon in the 1950's. If you wanted the best, you went to Maxwell. He observed that oftentimes his patients' unhappiness and insecurities were not cured after the surgery even though they believed that the procedure would cure them.

A person with a damaged nose might think, "If only my nose wasn't crooked, I would be confident and happy." Sometimes after the surgery this happened and sometimes it did not.

Maltz realized that people oftentimes see themselves inaccurately and that their perceptions are based on inaccurate beliefs that are embedded in their non-conscious. In other words, due to what was inside their heads, people were unable to objectively see themselves. Their internal self-image did not correspond to their external image.

Sometimes a patient would not even be able to see that he or she looked different after the procedure. Family and friends could see the difference but the individual's self image was so strong that he or she could not even see the change.

My understanding is that anorexic people see someone fat when they look in the mirror. They are able to objectively look at others to determine if they are overweight or not but they cannot objectively look at themselves. Crazy as this sounds, we all do some version of this where we do not objectively see ourselves.

Maltz realized that he needed to treat the "internal scars" at least as much as he treated the external scars.

Maltz's book, "Psycho Cybernetics" was a pioneering book in the field of personal growth and awareness.

In order to attract something different from what you already have, you will need to heal some of your "internal scars". You will need to change some of your non-conscious programming.

Your non-conscious programming is neither good nor bad. However, some of your programming supports you and some of it is in your way.

Non-conscious programming is an absolutely essential part of your life. If you had to stop, think about, and process every stimulus you would become immediately overwhelmed and unable to function. Your non-conscious programming allows most things to be taken care of on autopilot so that your conscious mind can cope.

Remember when you first learned to drive and how much you had to think about what you were doing? Now the majority of your driving is on autopilot. You just do it. You do not need to think about it and process what to do next. That is an example of how your non-conscious programming creates shortcuts that allow you to simply react without needing to first stop and process. You have thousands of these shortcuts.

This picture of my daughter, Sabine, really captures the relationship between the conscious and the non-conscious.

She is as happy as can be driving her shopping cart. She is busy spinning her steering wheel. Of course who really determines where we go in the store? I do, the guy pushing the cart.

Your non-conscious mind processes 11 million bits of information every second. Your conscious mind processes 40 bits per second. Almost one million times more information enters your head than your conscious can perceive.

The reticular activation system is part of your non-conscious. It acts like your own personal Google search engine. It sorts through every one of those 11 million actions every second and determines which 40 of those make it to your consciousness. Things deemed important get sent to the conscious mind and the rest, the vast majority, remain non-conscious.

Surely you have had the experience of hearing something from across the room that caught your attention. Your non-conscious had been hearing that conversation the whole time it was going on even though you had not consciously heard a word of it. However, when something relevant was said, it triggered your reticular activation system and that bit of information got routed to your consciousness and thus you were able to hear it.

When my wife was pregnant, I saw pregnant women everywhere I turned. It really freaked me out. They were everywhere. Of course, pregnant women have always been around. They just were not something that was particularly relevant to me until my wife became pregnant.

So, like it or not, you and your consciousness are not in charge of your life. Your non-conscious programming is! The good news is that contrary to popular opinion, change can be a quick easy process.

In the next chapter, you will learn an easy method to change your non-conscious programming.

How to make this part of your world

❖ Notice how patterned your life is.
  ◻ Which shoe do you put on first?
  ◻ How you respond to certain situations?
  ◻ What things do you do and what things don't you do?

❖   Brush your teeth with your opposite hand and see what you notice. It is still you brushing your teeth but it sure will not feel that way.

❖   Notice repetitive patterns in others. If they have them you must have them too.

Chapter 18

DIYHTR

Conventional wisdom says that it is a long, hard, slow, difficult and sometimes painful process to change who you are. Traditional methods spend years trying to create these kinds of changes. However, change can happen much faster than that as this story about the birth of Thought Form Therapy illustrates.

Roger Callahan, a clinical psychologist, was working with a client of his named Mary. Mary had a severe phobia of water. In fact, she had never even given her own children a bath because you have to use water to do that. She had nightmares several times a week about water taking her away. Obviously her life was severely impacted by this phobia.

They were doing a type of therapy where Mary would sit in a chair and look at a swimming pool off in the distance. The idea behind this was that Mary would just get so overwhelmed with her experience of water that she would be okay with water.

One day while they were doing this, Mary happened to mention how upset her stomach was. Dr. Callahan had a flash of inspiration at this moment. He remembered seeing on an acupuncture chart that the stomach meridian starts just beneath the eye. (A meridian is roughly equivalent to your arteries and veins. Your arteries and veins move blood around your body and your meridians move energy around your body.)

Dr. Callahan told Mary to start tapping on the bone just under her eye. After a couple of minutes Mary jumped out of her chair and started running towards the pool. Thinking that she might hurt herself, he yelled, "STOP!" Mary yelled back over her shoulder, "don't worry I know that I don't know how to swim." She ran to the edge of the pool and started splashing water on her face.

It was the summertime and afternoon thunder clouds were rolling in. Normally, this would cause Mary to have a panic attack. She drove to the beach and waded in the ocean during a thunderstorm before she went home for the evening.

Dr. Callahan was left to figure out, "What just happened here". He concluded that maybe some of the things about ourselves that we believe are permanent or difficult to change are nothing more than stuck energy patterns.

Dr. Callahan wrote a book called *"The Five-Minute Phobia Cure"*. Using his protocols literally thousands of people have been cured of their phobias in less than five minutes.

Think of it this way. If there is a big rock in a stream, there will always be a disturbance in the water around that rock. The only way to get rid of the disturbance is to remove the rock. Once the rock is removed the water can flow smoothly.

We have lots of rocks, our non-conscious programming, in the middle of our energy streams that create a continual disturbance. When we remove these rocks, change can happen really fast.

One day I was having coffee with a client. He mentioned that he was good at sales but not at closing. When he said the part about not being able to close, out of the corner of my eye I saw a disturbance in his energy field. I was so excited I almost threw my cup across the coffee shop. I saw the energetic disruption that stood between this guy and him being an effective closer.

Even though I have seen human energy for a long time, I had never seen an energy disruption like that.

Once I learned to see the disruptions, I was able to create a very simple system for removing them, **DIYHTR**. Now whether you can see these energetic disruptions or not, you can remove them.

DIYHTR

DIYHTR stands for **Do It Yourself - Head Trash Removal.** It is a system for identifying and then clearing out the non-conscious programming that is in your way of getting what you want.

When you have a conscious desire or intention that is not in harmony with your non-conscious programming, it is very difficult to achieve that desire or intention. This is because the non-conscious processes are in charge, not your conscious desires and intentions.

DIYHTR creates alignment between the conscious and the non-conscious thus making it much more likely that you will achieve your dreams, goals and desires.

Your body is an amazing feedback device. It can easily show you where these disconnects or short circuits are between your conscious desires and intentions and your non-conscious conditioning and programming. All you have to do is say a statement out loud and then pay attention to what you notice. Your body will respond to what you say.

For example, imagine that it is your desire to be an excellent salesperson. So, you say out loud, "It is okay for me to be an excellent salesperson". Then you notice what you notice. Did that statement feel believable? Did it come out smoothly or did your throat constrict? Did that statement seem true? Did the little voice in the back of your head comment, "No it's not!"? Was there any other sort of disconcerting reaction?

If you experienced any sort of adverse reaction then you know that you have non-conscious programming that is in conflict with the statement you made.

If the statement came out smoothly and easily and seems totally believable then you know that your non-conscious programming and your conscious desire are in alignment.

Once you have identified a conflict between your non-conscious programming and your conscious desire, you can then change the non-conscious programming to come into alignment with your conscious desire.

The steps to changing your non-conscious programming

1)   Say your statement out loud and see how your body responds to it. If there is an adverse response, continue with step number two.

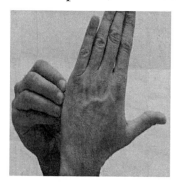

2)   Keeping your statement in mind, tap on the karate chop point of either hand for about 30 seconds. Tap tap tap tap

3)   Keeping the statement in mind, tap on the bone beneath your eyes for about 30 seconds. Tap tap tap tap

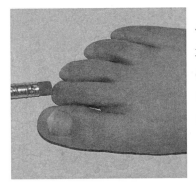

4) Keeping the statement in mind, tap on the outside edge of the toenail of your second toe for about 30 seconds. Tap tap tap tap

5) Keeping the statement in mind, tap on the karate chop point again and this time **slowly** roll your eyes from the floor up to the ceiling. Only move your eyes, not your head. Tap tap tap tap

6) Say your statement out loud again. If it feels strong, you have successfully cleared the non-conscious programming. If it feels better but does not feel 100% strong then go through the procedure again.

7) Repeat the above with related statements. For example if your original statement was, "It is okay for me to grow my business." You would also want to test: "I deserve to grow my business." "I am able to grow my business." "I enjoy growing my business." "It is safe to grow my business." "I can see myself growing my business." "I choose to grow my business." And anything else that comes to mind. This way you are covering all the angles around that issue.

Let us practice. Remember Chapter 12, where we talked about the importance of being able to receive compliments?

Say out loud, "It is okay for me to deeply and completely receive compliments about what a wonderful human being I am."

Note your response to this. On a scale of one to ten how believable was it?

Now do the **DIYHTR** process on this statement.

After you have completed **DIYHTR** say the same statement out loud again. Notice that you have a different experience of yourself. The statement will feel more truthful, more real, and more believable.

This is so important to get! You have just changed your non-conscious programming; you have just changed the stuff that goes on inside your head, which will make it easier for you to accept compliments. Most people in the world do not know or believe that change can happen this quickly. But, it can and just did! The fact that you felt different the second time you said the statement is proof that something changed.

Now if it felt better but not a 10, then you need to go through the process again. You also need to make a bunch of related statements like: "I'm able to... ", "I deserve to..." and so on.

DIYHTR is incredibly powerful. However for it to work, you have to use it. I teach this to people when I give talks. Every so often I run into someone who tells me that they have been using what I taught them and invariably they have created change in their lives.

In Chapter 15, The Magic of Intention, in the "how to make this part of your world" section, I mentioned that you will learn a technique that will make you more effective in using intention. That technique is **DIYHTR** and you can use it on the following statements.

It is okay to be in charge of my life.

It is okay to be responsible for creating the life I want.

It is okay to influence the way my life turns out.

It is okay for me to set strong intentions.

It is okay for me to have my hands on the "steering wheel of my life".

Remember to come at these from a bunch of different angles. "I'm able to...", "I deserve to...", "It is safe to..." and so on.

In the areas of your life where you are not getting the results that you want, start making statements about them out loud. Pay attention to your body and you will soon discover where your non-conscious programming is in conflict with the statements you are making. Do **DIYHTR** on these statements.

Appendix 1 has a list of statements to clear if you need some assistance in getting started with using **DIYHTR**.

How to make this part of your world

❖　Use **DIYHTR**. Use it a lot.

❖　Make statements out loud about the areas of your life where you are not getting the results you desire. When you discover a conflict between the conscious and non-conscious, use **DIYHTR.**

❖　Work through the list of statements to clear in Appendix 1, especially if you are not sure where to start using **DIYHTR**.

Chapter 19

The Sand Technique

The most important part about the tapping in **DIYHTR** is your intention. When you get clear on why you are doing the tapping and what it is supposed to do, then you can do it even faster.

The tapping is a method for dissolving a persistent energy blockage. This blockage has a meaning and acts as a limit on what is possible.

Sand is a really good analogy for what happens in your energy field. When sand gets wet and then dries out, it can clump up into little chunks that look like rocks. But when you pick up one of these "rocks" and rub it in your hands, it immediately turns back into sand.

This is exactly what happens in your energy field. The disruptions in your energy field are like the clumps of sand. In the stuckness of the energy lies its meaning. As soon as the energy becomes unstuck, the meaning disappears.

Keeping the sand example in mind, you can do the same thing with your non-conscious programming. You can imagine that the programming is right in between your hands. Then all you need to do is rub your hands together and intend that you are dis -

integrating the stuck energy. Then blow on your hands to further disperse the energy.

The Steps to
Using the Sand Technique

1)   Say your statement out loud and see how your body responds to it. If there is an adverse response, continue with step number two.

2)   Imagine that the non-conscious programming is between your hands. Briskly rub you hands together just like you would with that clump of sand.

3)   Then blow on your hands like you would blow the sand out of your hands.

4).   Do steps 2 and 3 three times

5).   Say your statement out loud again. If it feels strong, you have successfully cleared the non-conscious programming. If it feels better but does not feel 100% strong then go through the procedure again.

6).   Repeat the above with related statements.

This is just like **DIYHTR** except that instead of tapping in the four different places, you are rubbing your hands together and then blowing on them. It is faster than **DIYHTR**.

How to make this
part of your world

❖   Use this technique after you have practiced **DIYHTR**. Use it when you have become comfortable with **DIYHTR** and with the intentions behind **DIYHTR**.

Chapter 20

Choosing Your Results

There is an enormous difference between wanting something and actively choosing it. Say out loud, "I want to be happy." Then say, "I choose to be happy. Can you feel the difference?

The act of choosing is one of the most powerful, if not the most powerful, actions you can take as a human being. "I choose!" Those are words of power.

You can use **DIYHTR**, other techniques and methods, and do all kinds of clearing so that you are open to the possibility of what you want. However, until you actively choose that result, it just remains a possibility.

That is why one of the statements that I recommend clearing around in **DIYHTR** is: "I choose to _____."

Here is an analogy. Think about dating. You could do all kinds of work so that you are clear and open to the possibility of having a sweetheart. However, at some point you have to say, "I choose you" and then ask that person out on a date. Once you have done that you move from the possibility of dating into the reality of dating. After you have dated around for a while, you will probably choose one person and get married.

Create a morning ritual around choice. Have a few statements that you say when you start your day about the kind of life you choose for yourself. This gives you an awesome context from which to live your day. For example: I choose great happiness! I choose to have money be my friend! I choose to have a deep, loving, supportive and playful relationship with my significant other! I choose to live a great life!

My personal favorite is to choose to experience great joy in my day.

Try it. This is a very powerful way to start your day.

How to make this part of your world

❖ Take a look at your goals, dreams and desires. Have you chosen them? If not, powerfully choose them.

❖ Start your day with an "I choose _____!" statement.

Chapter 21

The Collapse

One of the most destructive ways that people get in their own way on a non-conscious level is the either/or collapse. When this happens two independent statements get collapsed together into one belief. This belief usually has an either/or choice that has to be made. Instead of having many options, things become black and white. It is either this or that – end of discussion.

Here is how that looked for one of my clients who was struggling to get her career going. She had collapsed these two thoughts into one statement: Either I can be a good wife and mother, or I can make a lot of money. So at a non conscious level she had to choose. "Do I want to be a good wife and mother or do I want to be a successful business woman and make money?" Obviously she could do both but because she had collapsed these two statements together, she could not have both.

If she were being a good wife and mother, which is her number one priority, then her non-conscious programming would not allow her to be successful in business. Furthermore, this collapse continually provided guilt. Any time she would focus on her business, she would feel guilty about not being a good mother and wife.

The only place that this either/or is really true is in her non-conscious programming. It is not a universal truth, it is something that got made up and became true for her. We were able to switch the either/or to an and/both. "I can be both a good wife and mother and a successful business woman who earns good money." Once we did that, it became possible for her to have both where before it was impossible for her to have both.

When you identify these kinds of linked beliefs in your life, you can use **DIYHTR** to change that limiting programming.

How to make this
part of your world

❖ Look for the collapses in your programming and then use **DIYHTR** to separate them.

Chapter 22

Conflicting Wants and Beliefs

Closely related to the either/or collapse is the dilemma of conflicting wants. This is when you have a conscious desire and directly opposed to this is a desire that you are not aware of, a desire that is below the surface. So you have conflicting agendas within you, and a tug of war going on. Usually the desire outside of your awareness is the stronger of the two. So you end up battling yourself and not getting what you think you want.

A client of mine had a ski weekend planned and her condo already rented. Then some circumstances changed and she had to call off her ski trip. She wanted me to assist her in clearing out whatever was in the way so that she could use the Law of Attraction to get a full refund on the condo.

In her case, the desire outside of her awareness (to still go on this skiing trip) was far stronger than the desire she was aware of (to get her money back). I had to point this out a few times before she was able to see the other desire and really "get" it.

From there she now had possibility. She could let go of the one desire (it does not matter which one) and then focus on the other. With this conflict gone, she was no longer tearing herself up inside.

Another client had been doing at lot of work on shifting her limiting money programming. However, she was not seeing any results. She had these two conflicting beliefs: I am a good person. It is bad to have debt. So since she has debt, how can she be a good person? Basically she had put herself into a no win situation. The facts are that in this moment she has debt. If it is bad to have debt then how can she possibly be a good person?

With this playing in the background, any Law of Attraction work she did around money was taking place on top of her feeling bad about herself. After all, she had debt and therefore she must be a bad person; any Law of Attraction work she would do around money would trigger this feeling bad about her. As I am sure you remember your feelings are crucial in being able to attract what you want.

For her, using the "even though I have debt, I deeply love and approve of myself." technique that we covered in Chapter 7 enabled her to disentangle these two beliefs.

Both of these examples illustrate the importance of digging down a little and really being honest with yourself about what you want. When you get clear about that, then you can move forward.

When you do not do this, you are doing damage to yourself by pretending to want something that you really do not want while denying a deeper desire.

How to make this part of your world

❖ When you are not getting what you want, dig down a little deeper and see if there is a conflicting agenda. If there is, resolve that conflict through:

   ☐ **DIYHTR** (Chapter 18)
   ☐ Loving yourself (Chapter 7)
   ☐ The Cesar Millan Relax Technique to let go of one of the alternatives (Chapter 11)
   ☐ Actively and powerfully choosing one of the alternatives

Chapter 23

The Grand Canyon Effect

When people talk about their goals, dreams and intentions I often see what I call the Grand Canyon Effect. They see what they want as being far removed from them. Often, they see it as far away and even unattainable.

It looks sort of like this.

To get from one side of the canyon where you are, all the way over to the other side of the canyon where your bars of gold are, looks at best like really hard work. It might even look completely impossible.

You can gaze longingly over the canyon at the gold you probably will never get because it is too far away and there is too much work between you and it. This produces the feelings and experience of "wanting" not of "having". You are probably not inspired to jump into immediate action.

The solution to this is to make the Grand Canyon disappear, to ground you in your goal, dream, or intention. Once the canyon has squeezed together and disappeared, the gold will be right at your feet.

Before we get into the steps to do this, we need to cover two background ideas.

Remember in Chapter 7, how you turned on the "happiness" light switch in the center of your chest. You will be turning on two light switches in this exercise. One is located between your eyes and the other is located at your throat.

The switch between your eyes turns on qualities like: vision, clarity, will power, focus and meaning.

The switch at your throat turns on qualities like: the ability to ask for what you want, the ability to receive, self expression, communication and the power of the spoken word.

The second background idea comes from the Star Wars movie. In the movie, the little droid, R2D2, projected a beam of light out of his head that produced a hologram of Princess Leia. You will be projecting a beam of light out of the space between your eyes and your throat. These two beams will meet about one foot in front of you and form an image of your goal, dream or desire.

The steps to disappear the
Grand Canyon and ground your intention

1)   Get clear about what you want. Be specific.

2)   Get yourself into a high-energy state of being. You could do an inventory of all you have to be grateful for. You could think of someone you deeply love. You could dance or sing. Get yourself feeling juicy.

3)   Close your eyes. Bring your attention to the space between your eyes. Intend it to bloom wide open and then turn on your focus, clarity and vision.

4)   Bring your attention to your throat. Intend that it blooms wide open and then turn on the ability to clearly and powerfully ask for what you want. Also turn on your ability to easily receive that which you ask for.

5)   Now project a beam of light from each of these two energy centers that meet a foot in front of your face to create a 3D image of what you want. Bring in focus, clarity, vision, intention and the power of the spoken word. Do this for 30 seconds, or longer if your image does not seem strong or clear. Have the image continue to get stronger, brighter and clearer.

6) Bring the image inside of your head and bless it with spiritual connection, guidance, and alignment from the top of your head.

7) Then bless it with focus, vision, meaning and clarity from the space between your eyes.

8) Move the image down to your throat and bless it with asking for what you want, self-expression, communication, creativity, the ability to receive and the power of the spoken word.

9) Move the image down to your heart and bless it with love, joy, courage, confidence and strong intention.

10) Move the image down to your solar plexus and bless it with flow and appropriateness.

11) Move the image down to your navel and bless it with centeredness, intuition and excitement.

12) Move the image down into your pelvis and bless it with passion, connectedness, belonging and relatedness.

13) Move the image down to the tip of your spine and bless it with self-trust, security, vitality and energy.

14) Move the image down your legs, through the soles of your feet and into the earth. With each exhale move the image closer to the center of the earth.

15) When it feels right, release the image and open your eyes.

After you do this, you will most likely notice how much more real and believable your goal, dream or desire feels.

You will probably also feel very centered, peaceful and quiet. Besides grounding your intention, this exercise also energetically balances your whole body.

This is a great exercise to do on a daily basis.

How to make this part of your world

❖   Do this exercise daily.

Chapter 24

Agreements

An agreement is a mutual understanding or arrangement. If you and I have an agreement to meet for lunch this Friday at 12:30 at Willy's Cantina, we both better be there or else there will be a "problem". We are both expecting each other to do certain things based on our agreement. If those things do not get done then our expectations are not met and there are consequences.

Legal documents are often referred to as binding agreements. There is a major consequence if the agreement is broken.

You have made agreements at a non-conscious level. Chances are that these agreements exist completely outside of your awareness. You made them as a survival or coping strategy. This sort of agreement is a lose-lose arrangement.

You agree to give something up and in return another person is supposed to give you something or act in a certain way. The problem is that the only place this agreement took place was inside your head. The other person never actually agreed to uphold their end of the agreement. Consequently you give something up and do not get anything back in return. You lose twice.

Here is how that looked for one of my clients whose career requires that she speaks in public frequently and is able to inspire people. She came to see me because her results were not as good as she knew they could be.

We discovered that she had a non-conscious agreement with her father. She agreed to give up being self-expressed and be a good quiet girl and in return she would get more love and attention from her father. Of course, her father never actually agreed to this so she ended up limiting her self-expression and got nothing in return for this. The only place that this agreement was created and agreed to was inside her head. Furthermore, she had no idea that she had made this agreement in the first place or that she was still bound by it. This all took place at a non-conscious level.

As you can imagine, needing to inspire people and being limited in self-expression do not go well together. Once we replaced this agreement with one that supported her (something along the lines of: it is safe for me to be a great communicator), she experienced a shift in her effectiveness as a communicator.

The only thing these self-imposed agreements do is limit you. When you remove them, you create freedom.

A friend of mine noticed that as soon as she turned 40 she started getting bigger, especially her derriere.

She knows about agreements. She explored and discovered that she had an agreement with herself that after 40 women started to get fat. She had noticed this in her mother and in her mother's friends and at a non-conscious level made this her truth.

She broke this agreement and easily lost 12 pounds within two weeks. She noticed herself wanting to eat a little healthier and wanting to walk more. She changed with ease once she broke the limiting agreement.

Here is an agreement that I had that was very much in my way. My friend, Allison Taylor (**Paravox.com**) helped me to see this agreement. Allison is a practitioner of PSYCH-K, which is a great system for changing beliefs and non-conscious programming. We get together once a month and work with each other's businesses.

One day she said to me, "You have a client package called The Inevitable Success Program. Inevitable Success is a bold claim. However, you do not seem that bold when you talk about this program. You seem to be holding back. What is that all about?"

We uncovered an agreement between my father and me.

One day when I was a little kid, my dad was leaving for work. He said to me, "Bye bye, my little lamb."

I replied, "Bye bye, rooster."

For whatever reasons, my dad got mad. He thought it was disrespectful of me to call him a name and he let me know about it. Then he let me know about it some more.

I was devastated. I crawled under the dining room table and cried my eyes out. It seemed so unfair! He was being playful with me. I played back and got into trouble.

I made an agreement at that moment. "I will give up being bold and self-expressed. In turn, dad will love me and that scene will never repeat itself."

My ability to boldly express myself was compromised by one joke I made as a little kid. I gave something up, bold self-expression, got nothing back in return and had no idea that I had made this agreement.

What have you agreed to but did not know that you have agreed to?

Discovering Agreements

It really is simple to discover these agreements. All you need to do is get quiet and ask yourself. The answer will come.

Take a look at your life and see where your results are not what you want. Ask yourself, "Have I made any agreements that are affecting _____?"

If the answer is "no" then you are done. If the answer is "yes" then ask yourself, "what is the agreement?" Then wait for the answer.

Breaking Agreements

Once you have discovered an agreement that does not serve you, you will want to break that agreement and create a new one.

To break the agreement, you can use **DIYHTR**. Imagine that you agreed not to be self-expressed. Then, use **DIYHTR** on "it is okay to be self expressed" and so on.

You can also visualize that the agreement is written out and that this is the only written copy in the entire universe. You can either run the paper through a paper shredder or else throw it into a bonfire. Then verbally declare that agreement null, void and officially broken.

Now it is time to make a new agreement. Create an agreement with yourself that works for you.

My client who does public speaking made a new agreement with herself to be an effective powerful public speaker. My friend who put on weight made a new agreement with herself to be healthy and fit. I made a new agreement with myself to be boldly self-expressed.

It does not matter what your new agreement is as long as it works for you.

How to make this
part of your world

❖   When you are not getting what you want, look for agreements. Break those agreements and create new agreements that support you.

Chapter 25

Final Notes

The Law of Attraction is an amazing beautiful tool. However, a tool is only useful if you use it. As you have seen, each chapter ends with a section on "how to make this part of your life". These are specific actions you can take to assist you in integrating these tips, tools and techniques into your daily life.

The more that you can make these practices a habit, the more successful you will be. Routines and memory links are great ways to support yourself in doing this.

A routine is something that you do regularly at a regular time and at a specific place. One routine that I recommend is to spend two minutes thinking about what you have to be grateful for. Do this when you first wake up and again just before you go to sleep.

A memory link is something that serves as a reminder. It links a common activity to something else. For example, you might want to visualize what you want every time you brush your teeth. Your toothbrush then becomes a stimulus to remind you to visualize what you want. You might even tape a note to the bathroom mirror to help remind you as you go about creating this habit.

You do not need to do everything in this book. In fact, I know that you will not. However, even if you take just one of these tips, tools, or techniques and really consistently apply it in your life, it will make a difference.

I believe that you are here on earth to live a marvelous, joyful and happy life. The Law of Attraction can be a great tool to support you in doing that.

Remember that ultimately the Law of Attraction is about you loving and appreciating yourself more.

Be patient and loving with yourself. Be grateful.

Sometimes change occurs in a big jump and sometimes it occurs in small steps over time. Be ready for both. Stay curious and notice what is different.

When I go out of town and do not see my daughter for a few days, I am always surprised by how much she has changed. When I am at home, it is harder to notice these changes unless I look for them. When I look back, I can see that Sabine was not doing or could not do this a week ago but now she can.

Look at yourself this same way and see the changes that you have made. Be generous with yourself!

When you are stuck, cannot seem to change, and are not getting what you want, get assistance. There are a lot of people who can help you get out of your own way at a non-conscious level. Use them!

I have found the work that I do (obviously), PSYCH-K, NLP, EFT, TFT and hypnosis to all be powerful tools. Find a practitioner in one of these disciplines and have them assist you.

One final thought: human beings are incredibly complex. There are so many factors at play in any one moment, including the divine, that it is impossible to know what causes what. Love and be gentle with yourself even if the Law of Attraction does not seem to be getting you what you want.

I wish you great joy in your life!

Love,
Jonathan

Appendix 1

Statements to Clear Using DIYHTR

Here is a list of statements to clear that will help you get started using this powerful tool.

With each of these statements, say them out loud and pay attention to your physical, mental and emotional responses. Clear the ones that need clearing. With each statement, approach it several different ways: It is okay to be... ; I am able to be... ; I deserve to be... ; It is safe to be... ; I see myself as... ; I am... ; I choose to...

- ❖ a success
- ❖ grow my business
- ❖ a wise savvy business person
- ❖ an entrepreneur
- ❖ the authority in and about my life
- ❖ to stand up for myself
- ❖ to be happy
- ❖ alive and here on planet earth *(this is an issue for some people)*
- ❖ ask for what I want
- ❖ willing to let other people help you – really help you
- ❖ receive

- to get what I want
- to play big
- to have other's assist me
- to act in my own best interest
- to say "no"
- to be told "no"
- to sell
- to sell my own products and/or services
- to make money
- to have money
- to be wealthy
- to have fun making money
- make money with ease
- to effectively manage my money
- to grow my money
- to have money be my friend
- to not meet other's expectations
- to play full out
- to put myself on the line
- to be visible
- to assume total responsibility for my life
- accomplish anything I desire
- know that the world is safe
- know that I am okay
- to be self-expressed

Appendix 2

Recommended Resources

The following are my suggestions. These are resources that I have used, enjoyed and found valuable. Many of them could be listed in more than one category. I put them where they seemed to fit best.

Law of Attraction
Books:

The Secret
> by Rhonda Byrne ISBN: 1582701709

Ask and It Is Given
> by Esther & Jerry Hicks ISBN: 1401904599

The Attractor Factor
> by Joe Vitale ISBN: 0470009802

The Spontaneous Fulfillment of Desire
> by Deepak Chopra ISBN: 1400054311

Excuse Me, Your Life is Waiting
> by Lynn Grabhorn ISBN: 1571743812

How To Create Gold: A Step-By-Step Method
> by Joyce M. Morris ISBN: 0978712102

DVD's:

The Secret

Websites:

smart-attractor.com

Mindset
Books:

God Wants You to be Rich
> by Paul Zane Pilzer ISBN: 1416549277

Loving What Is
> by Byron Katie ISBN: 0609608746

Radical Forgiveness: Making Room for the Miracle
> by Colin C. Tipping ISBN: 0970481411

Spiritual Power Tools
> by Lee Milteer ISBN: 1571744282

Websites:

masterminding101.com
> by Mary Robinson Reynolds

Working With the Non-Conscious
Books:

The Street Kid's Guide to Having It All
> by John Assaraf ISBN: 0972621423

Five Minute Phobia Cure
> by Roger Callahan Ph.D. ISBN: 0913864897

Using Your Brain for a Change
> by Richard Bandler ISBN: 0911226273

Frogs Into Princes
> by Richard Bandler and John Grinder ISBN: 0911226192

My Voice Will Go With You: The Teaching Tales of Milton H. Erickson
> by Sidney Rosen ISBN: 0393301354

Debug Your Mental Software
> by Jay Arthur ISBN: 1884180302

Psycho Cybernetics
> by Maxwell Maltz ISBN: 0671700758

The User Illusion: Cutting Consciousness Down to Size
by Tor Norretranders ISBN: 0140230122
The 11th Element: The Key to Unlocking Your
Master Blueprint for Wealth and Success
by Robert Scheinfeld ISBN: 0471444138

Websites:
emofree.com   Emotional Freedom Technique
brainbullet.com

Intention
Books:
The Power of Intention: Learning to Co-Create Your
World Your Way
by Wayne Dyer ISBN: 1401902162
DVD's:

Shackleton
The Endurance: Shackleton's Legendary Antarctic
Expedition

Quantum Physics
Books:
The Dancing Wu Li Masters
by Gary Zukav ISBN: 0060959681
The Tao of Physics
by Fritjof Capra ISBN: 1570625190
DVD's & VHS:
What The Bleep Do We Know Anyway
Mindwalk

Other
Books:

Zero Limits
> by JoeVitale ISBN: 0470101474

The Field
> by Lynne Mc Taggart ISBN: 006143518X

You Can Heal Your Life
> by Louise L. Hay ISBN: 0937611018

Cesar's Way: The Natural Everyday Guide to
Understanding & Correcting Common Dog Problems
> by Cesar Millan ISBN: 0307337332

Appendix 3

About the Author

Jonathan Manske is a **Cerebral Sanitation Engineer**.

Jonathan speaks professionally, delivers corporate training and does private consulting on issues related to taking out your Head Trash, productivity, under performance and helping people to get what they really want.

Jonathan has spent over 20 years really studying people. He has learned to look at people as an energy system. From this point of view, he can literally see the limiting beliefs, limiting perspectives and other Head Trash in your energy field. In response to what he sees, he has developed many tools and strategies to deal with

Head Trash and create meaningful change.

Jonathan's mission is to serve, elevate and inspire ~ to end the suffering caused by Head Trash and to support people to live rich, fulfilling and enjoyable lives.

Most people know that belief, mindset, self-image and attitude are a huge part of the success formula. They know the importance of working on themselves and know what they need to do to upgrade these areas. However, knowing what to do and actually doing it on a consistent basis are two different things. This book is a "how to" of tools and strategies for doing your personal growth work and provides a workbook to support you in doing your work on a daily basis.

Personal growth is not rocket science; the key lies in doing the work daily. This book supports you to do just that.

Most people believe praise, appreciation, and compliments are great ways to motivate and inspire people. Many think these communication tools are good people skills and are useful everywhere ~ from parenting to the boardroom, from friendship to leadership, from relationships to coaching. People mistakenly believe these tools are the keys to unlock human potential.

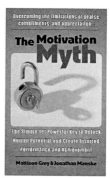

In this provocative and compelling book, Grey and Manske debunk the myth that performance, achievement, confidence, and connection ~ at work, at school, and at home ~ are improved by these communication tools.

Fortunately, there is an alternative, acknowledgement. This communication tool is the cure for underperformance, lack of self-confidence, and ineffective motivation techniques. Acknowledgement changes lives!

From Under Performance To Superior Performance

Bring in Jonathan to train, inspire and elevate your organization. Jonathan can help you create in-house programs to create greater productivity, greater job satisfaction, and programs to develop the mindset, beliefs and attitudes necessary for success.

❖ ❖ ❖ ❖ ❖

Ask Jonathan to speak at your next event!

❖ ❖ ❖ ❖ ❖

Call Jonathan at

303.552.7285

or visit

JonathanManske.com

Are You Serious
About Your Success?

Would you like to get out of
your own way and get more
of what you really want?

Jonathan does private consulting on issues
related to taking out your Head Trash,
productivity, under performance and assisting you
to get what you really want.

Give him a call at 303.552.7285 or
e-mail jonathan@jonathanmanske.com

Discuss what working with a
Cerebral Sanitation Engineer could do for you.

(Note: Work over the phone is
just as effective as in person.)

This work is also available
to small groups in
Manske's Momentum Programs.

JonathanManske.com